THE BIBLE'S BEST LOVE STORIES

To Mary Jane,

With Peace, Joy & Love,

Allen Flughy

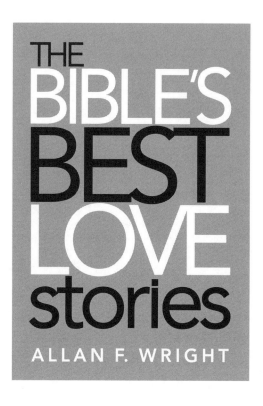

THE
BIBLE'S
BEST
LOVE
stories

ALLAN F. WRIGHT

ST. ANTHONY MESSENGER PRESS
Cincinnati, Ohio

Scripture passages have been taken from *New Revised Standard Version Bible*, copyright ©1989 by the Division of Christian Education of the National Council of the Churches of Christ in the U.S.A., and used by permission. All rights reserved.

Cover and book design by Mark Sullivan
Cover images © istockphoto.com | Diana Walters | Rakoskerti

LIBRARY OF CONGRESS CATALOGING-IN-PUBLICATION DATA
Wright, Allan F., 1964-
The Bible's best love stories / Allan F. Wright.
p. cm.
ISBN 978-86716-960-7 (alk. paper)
1. Love—Biblical teaching. I. Title.
BS680.L64W75 2010
241'.4—dc22

2010019434

ISBN 978-0-86716-960-7

Published by St. Anthony Messenger Press
28 W. Liberty St.
Cincinnati, OH 45202
www.AmericanCatholic.org
www.SAMPBooks.org

Printed in the United States of America.

Printed on acid-free paper.

10 11 12 13 14   5 4 3 2 1

To Desiree, Sophia, Cataleen, and Abigail
The Great Love Stories of My Life

"Nothing attracts like love…love and you will win every heart"
—Blessed Pauline Von Mallinckrodt,
founder of the Sisters of Christian Charity

LDM
Laudetur Deo Mariaeque
"Praise to God and to Mary"

contents

acknowledgments

I would like to thank all those who have modeled love for me in my life, and those who through their love, support and encouragement in my vocation as disciple, husband, and father: First of all to Ivan and Jane Wright, my mom and dad, what a blessing you continue to be in my life; to Nina and Chris, Cheri, Charlie, to David and Diane. In grateful appreciation to Amber Dolle who lovingly took time to "look things over" for me and to provide feedback on this project; to her husband, Nick, and sons, John Paul and Andrew; to Jordan and Trish, Kelsey, Paula, and Monroe, Shawn, Toni, Christine, and Cameron, and Dr. James Sulliman. To Dianne Traflet, J.D., S.T.D., to Diane Carr, to the Most Reverend Arthur J. Serratelli, S.T.D., S.S.L., D.D., for his love of Scripture and leadership within the diocese of Paterson, N.J. To the Demscak family, the Sisters of Christian Charity at Assumption College for Sisters, to Sr. Theresina, Sr. Mary Jo, Sr. Eileen, and Joan Dwyer at the House of Prayer who always reflect Christ's love through their hospitality. To Katie Carroll, who lovingly edited this book, and the staff at St. Anthony Messenger Press. Thanks to the Missionaries of Charity Sisters (Contemplative) in Plainfield, New Jersey. Your desire to give all to God, your joy, and your holiness make me a better man. To

Sister Mary Joseph Schultz, S.C.C., Ginger Kamenitzer and Father Geno Sylva at Saint Paul's Inside the Walls who give the new evangelization flesh and blood, spirit and life. To Mike and Cary Saint Pierre and their children: Grace, Thomas, and Ella—your friendship and faithfulness to Christ are always an inspiration. To Father Jim Chern, Jeff Lienhart, Roger and Sandy Wilkin, for their friendship. To Father Dennis Berry, S.T., PH.D. who, while far away, remains close to our hearts. To Sister Percylee Hart, R.S.M., and my friends at Union Catholic. To Monsignor Patrick Brown, pastor of Saint Vincent de Paul parish. To all who have answered God's call to the priesthood in this Year for Priests—may Saint John Vianney be your guide.

May your bridges all be 16'5" and your road be straight and smooth.

Love stories never go out of style. There is something about them that intrigues us. Whether it's on the stage, the big screen, in the pages of a juicy novel or in real life, we desire to enter into the story to see how it will turn out. Even when we have seen the movie once, we go back time and time again. No doubt a few of your favorites come to mind if you think for a minute or two.

Professional recording artist and friend Don Frio mentioned to me that there were roughly fourteen thousand recorded songs with the word *love* in the title and that list keeps growing every year. (Compare that to only 123 songs with the word *work* in the title!) Just think of the love songs we hear on the radio that have become favorites through the years. When we hear them we start singing along (at least I do!) and they often bring us back to a particular time and place in our lives.

The Bible has some pretty good love stories as well. While we may think of the Bible rather abstractly, the men and women to whom God revealed himself were no different than you and me in most ways. Our language, clothes, and cultural norms may differ and our cultural advances might make biblical characters appear too primitive for us to relate to. But to think that at their core they are radically different is misguided; I believe nothing could be further from the truth. These great love stories of the Bible involve people just like you and me. These are people who wanted to love and to be loved, they were people with passion, people who formed strong bonds of friendship, people who were loyal, people who had sexual desires, people who failed and received forgiveness, and people who strove to find God in their daily lives. Often they loved heroically, other times they failed miserably at loving the way God intended.

Throughout Scripture God communicates his love to us. He uses images of parenthood, marriage, weddings, adultery, and betrayal—some of the most powerful human experiences—in order to reveal divine love.

The foundational belief of Christianity is that God became flesh and lived among us. Christians believe that they have seen the face of love in the person of Jesus Christ. In light of God's revelation in Scripture and in the person of Jesus Christ, it is my hope that this book will allow you to enter into the lives of these characters, feel their emotions, and evaluate their choices so that you may experience real love that comes from God alone.

Allan F. Wright
Feast of the Holy Family

Before a Mass for the installation of a new pastor, a middle-aged woman came in to the sacristy and asked the bishop if he would offer a blessing for her parents, who were celebrating their anniversary that night. After Communion, the bishop invited the couple up, and these two older people started to walk slowly, carefully, up the aisle. For that procession, they never stopped holding each other's hands, and as they passed pew upon pew of people, filled with some family, but mostly parishioners, you could see their eyes filling with tears.

They arrived at the foot of the altar and the bishop asked them how many years they had been married? The wife responded "Sixty years today." The bishop followed up by asking them where they got married. The wife proudly responded, "Right here." There wasn't a dry eye in the church. The congregation began to clap and the bishop said, "You've been here in this parish for sixty years?" and the couple simply nodded their heads, as the wife said "We've been here every week since we were married."

That day no one could take their eyes off of this couple, yet, ironically, the two could barely look at each other. What was noticeable was the way they lovingly held hands throughout the entire blessing.

Observing this beautiful, rare sight, an outsider's curiosity was piqued: What had they lived through? What struggles, which must have seemed insurmountable at times, had they conquered? What joys and moments of pride, what sleepless nights of worry over their children had they endured? What twists and turns, ups and downs did they encounter? How often did they think, "That's it; I can't do this anymore"—and yet found the grace from God to give them the strength to try and return to that commitment they had made?

We don't have all the details of the intimate love story this couple shared. Witnessing the scene, you knew that you were in the presence of something sacred. Here were two imperfect people who kept trying, sixty years and counting, to live those radical, life-altering vows. And for those sixty years, they kept coming before that same altar in that same church. In moments of joy and sadness; milestones like a child's baptism or just another Sunday morning at Mass. We may not know all the details of their ongoing love story, but it was obvious to all those in that church just how active throughout their lives was the God who joined them together in marriage; he was, in fact, the key to its foundation.

While one can look at that true story and think how beautiful it is; I suspect for many there is sadness at the same time. Sadness that in our society marriage is often attacked and there is little expectation that the marriage vows last a lifetime. Sadness that in a culture where the love stories we view in popular movies or television shows seem to propose that such stories are the result of chance, fate, or luck for a few fortunate individuals (usually the most physically attractive people we've ever seen). For a lot of individuals, those fictitious stories are seen as more real than the one to which our anniversary couple bears witness.

The only way we'll be able to counteract these conflicting messages is by going back to basics, learning what a real love story is about.

Allan Wright has spent most of his adult life teaching and sharing the good news of Jesus. We get to enter the classroom with him as he teaches us what a real love story is. As in his previous works, *Silent Witnesses in the Gospels* and *Jesus in the House,* Allan brings fresh eyes to stories that are familiar to us. He reveals that the Scriptures contain countless genuine, heartfelt love stories —some of the greatest we have ever known. Stories not just of couples who entered into life-changing, life-giving relationships, but of men and women who laid down their lives for each other—and how those human relationships are a mere reflection of the extraordinary, radical, jealous love that God has for us, his precious creatures.

Father Jim Chern
Chaplain, Montclair State University
Feast of Saint Joseph

LOVE

IN

THE

OLD

TESTAMENT

When reading the Bible we come across customs and practices that are very often foreign from our own. Understanding these customs can offer a keen insight into the message that God communicates to his people in ways they can understand.

The Old Testament can be confusing because we don't have as many cultural insights to the time of the Jewish patriarchs as we do in the New Testament. The practice of polygamy and bigamy are examples of times when God seemed to remain silent in the face of sin.

It's important to remember that, until the children of Israel were freed from their slavery in Egypt and arrived at Mt. Sinai, the Ten Commandments had not yet been given. Thus, for example, When Abraham had a child by Sarah's maid, Hagar—the first recorded surrogate pregnancy—he was merely following the cultural norms of the time.

Another thing to consider is that, in these patriarchal societies, life for women was very difficult. Many women are mentioned in the Bible only in reference to their fathers, brothers, or husbands. The overwhelming majority of these nameless women were uneducated and had little skills with which to provide for themselves. A man who would take multiple wives could provide for and protect all of them. Living in a polygamist household may have been a better alternative than prostitution or slavery.

The Bible says that God's original intent was for marriage to exist between one man and one woman, "Therefore a man leaves his father and his mother and clings to his wife and they become one flesh" (Genesis 2:24). The teachings of Orthodox and Conservative Jewish communities, as well as the teachings of the Catholic church, are clear on this matter (*Catechism of the Catholic Church*, #1601–1654).

As is evident when reading the great loves stories of the Bible and other Old Testament texts, having a firm understanding of the time period, context, and culture does make the stories more understandable.

One of the most important tools in effective communication is trying to understand what the writer or speaker is saying. Words, both written and spoken, always carry meaning. Many of the words to which we attach a certain meaning are derived from our understanding of cultural norms. The meanings and nuances are often more caught than taught.

The Hebrew Bible—the Old Testament—was, of course, written in the Hebrew language. Scripture scholars, both Jewish and Christian, undertake the task of *exegesis,* that is, drawing out the meaning of the text that the author intended. This process can bring about different interpretations by different worshipping communities as they strive to understand what God is communicating through these human authors.

Vatican II's *Dei Verbum* speaks beautifully to our belief that God is the ultimate author of Scripture, and stresses the importance of interpreting God's message.

> However, since God speaks in Sacred Scripture through men in human fashion, the interpreter of Sacred Scripture, in order to see clearly what God wanted to communicate to us, should carefully investigate what meaning the sacred writers really intended, and what God wanted to manifest by means of their words (12).

It is with this understanding of the importance of words and their meaning that we are confronted with one of the Hebrew words for love: *ahava*. The word in Hebrew means "to give." Thus we understand *ahava* as "I give." *Ahava* is translated as a type of love that describes both love of God and interpersonal human love.

The word *hesed* or *chesed* is used some 248 times in the Bible. It is most often translated as *mercy* (149 times), *kindness* (40 times) and *loving kindness* (30 times). This word invokes the idea of a positive display of affection and care. *Hesed* is used many times to describe God's mercy. In the psalms we find *hesed* more often than in any other book in the Old Testament, approximately 125 times. The Lord's paths are described as mercy (Psalm 25:10), his loving-kindness is excellent, (Psalm 36:10), and mercy and truth have met together in the Lord (Psalm 86:5). These words illustrate that our God is one full of compassion and plenteous in mercy. (Psalm 86:15)

Various versions of the English Bible translate the word *hesed* as "unfailing love," "loving kindness," "mercy" and "loyalty." Often we see this word applied to the mercy of the Lord as articulated in God's covenant, which is ultimately an expression of mercy and love.

God is depicted in the Old Testament as full of *hesed*. The unchanging love, kindness, and mercy of God are shown to Israel throughout salvation history. The prophets said that God is worthy of praise because of his mercy. God's character, as revealed throughout Scripture, centers on his mercy, his loving-kindness, his *hesed*.

We also learn another Hebrew word, *rahamim*, which is the feminine voice of love. *hesed* highlights the marks of fidelity to self and of "responsibility for one's own love" while *rahamim*, in its very root, denotes the love of a mother (*rehem* is the word for "womb"). From the original bond and unity that links a mother to her child there springs a unique relationship, a particular love that it is completely gratuitous, not "earned." So *rahamim* generates a whole range of feelings, including goodness and tenderness, patience and understanding, that is, readiness to forgive.

Ahava, *hesed*, and *rahamim* further demonstrate that these words for love speak to our own human experiences. A true love is one that seeks another's best interest and goes beyond the requirements of justice. This type of love is powerful and life-changing and calls for a response.

chapter one

ADAM AND EVE
FIRST LOVE

The sstory of Adam and Eve has been the subject of more art-work, jokes, and cartoons than perhaps any other biblical narrative. The storyline is familiar to all: man and woman, the tree, the forbidden fruit, the serpent, and the fig leaves. These elements make Adam and Eve one of the most recognizable couples in history. It is within these passages from Genesis that we see the hand of God revealing his love for Adam and Eve, and God's will for couples throughout the ages.

"And God saw that it was good." This simple phrase, repeated no less than seven times in the first chapter of Genesis, provides affirmation from our Lord that creation is indeed good. In the same breath, God reveals that which is not good: "Then the LORD God said, 'It is not good that the man should be alone; I will make him a helper as his partner" (Genesis 2:18).

When a person is given a "helper" it implies that there is something lacking, something deficient. The "helper" is not subservient to the one they are helping, but rather they provide what is missing in the other. Together the two make the perfect match because each gives themselves to the other. Thus, a new union is formed.

We learn through the story of Adam and Eve that God literally divided man in half to form a partner for him. There was nothing deficient in Eve; she was exactly like Adam except for some creative differences, for God created them in the divine image (Genesis 1:27). Thus, Eve was the other half of Adam. Their bodies were designed to complement each other in more than just the physical relationship of the two becoming one. Eve made up for what was lacking in Adam, she completed him in all things.

In taking a wife, Adam would find completeness, oneness, and wholeness. What a joy that must have been for Adam after God had paraded all those animals in front of him! Adam finally knew he had found his "other self." Eve was the answer to his deepest longing, in her he found the meaning of his life and she for him. "Therefore a man leaves his father and his mother and clings to his wife and they become one flesh" (Genesis 2:24). Adam and Eve cannot be complete without the other.

The account of Adam and Eve is a love story, born in the heart of God and reflected in the flesh, bone, psyche, and breath of these two humans—the world's first lovers. Of course, we all know that this love story would soon become tragedy. Before we analyze what went wrong, let's go back to the beginning and see what went right.

Ah, finally Adam could give of himself completely; a perfectly compatible mate. One like himself—with a few differences—but oh how these differences were exhilarating to him! He could give of himself to the woman totally, in and through his body. Freely he can choose her; freely she can give herself to him. Faithfully he can love her alone and that love bears fruit in a child. This erotic love desires not just the conjugal union but desires the whole person. God desires this kind of love with us. This is a love that results in total communion.

In the same way God breathed life into Adam, the union of man and woman brings about new life as well. God set the stage, giving them to each other and putting them in the Garden of Eden. Their conjugal, self-giving love, modeled God's love for us. What could possibly go wrong?

Everything!

We read that God was walking in the garden in the cool of the day to ask Adam a vital question. It's natural to assume that God took this walk in the cool of the day each afternoon before the sun went down. I envision God delightfully listening to Adam and Eve's adventures and new discoveries with a smile on his face as they walked together, delighting in each other's company.

Things would soon change. In the garden where God settled Adam and Eve, Satan planted the seed of doubt. "Did God really tell you not to eat from any of the trees in the garden?" And then he lied, contradicting God. "You certainly will not die!" The result was not merely a broken command, but rather, broken relationships. Three in all were destroyed: Adam and Eve's relationship with God, their relationship with one another, and the interior relationships they had with themselves.

The first consequence we see in the garden is Adam and Eve's broken relationship with God. When we examine the story we see:

SIN

PRIDE

LUCIFER

What is the common thread in these three words? "I" rests in the center. Thus, we realize the crux of sin: putting "I" at the center of our lives, before others and before God.

Pride tells us that we know better than God; that we are better than others. When we believe this lie, chaos ensues. "I don't want to do what God says, I'm doing it my way." Saint Paul reminds us that the problem of sin is universal. "[A]ll have sinned and fall short of the glory of God" (Romans 3:23). Saint Paul will go on to say that what we receive from this choice, our wages for sin, is death (Romans 6:23).

Sin had a major impact on Adam and Eve's relationship with each other. What started out as ecstasy and total fulfillment ended up with each pointing their fingers at the other in blame. One has to wonder about Adam's role in the encounter with the serpent because we are told that, "...when the woman saw that the tree was good for food, and that it was a delight to the eyes, and that the tree was to be desired to make one wise, she took of its fruit and ate; and she also gave some to her husband, who was with her, and he ate" (Genesis 3:6). What was Adam thinking when all this was going on? He was at her side yet did nothing to protect his bride. No words of warning, no action to stop her from disobeying God? No confronting the serpent right in front of him? No call to God for assistance? What type of coward was he who would allow his wife to be deceived? Adam's failure to protect Eve was a failure to love.

After the fateful bite from the apple, God asks that beautiful, yet haunting question, "Where are you?" This is not a directional question such as, "Are you behind the tree or next to that rock?" Rather, it's a relational question. Where are you in relationship to me? Adam and Eve chose to hide from God, whereas God was seeking them. God never turns his back on us.

Finally we read that Adam and Eve covered themselves with fig leaves. Why cover themselves? They were created in the image and likeness of God, and, whatever God does, he does beautifully. With fear in their hearts, they were ashamed of what they had done. This shame translated into the realization that they were naked. The fig leaves with which they had covered themselves served as an external symbol of an internal problem: their fear and brokenness before God and each other.

I believe nothing much has changed since the time of Adam and Eve. When sin, as expressed in self-centeredness, arrogance and pride, enters the picture we still hide from God, act cowardly, blame one another, and even blame God for the world's faults. Today we simply cover ourselves with more clever and sophisticated adornments than fig leaves! Because of sin, we don't want people to see who we truly are—flawed humans. We attempt to escape the reality of our sins by defining and covering ourselves with things and accomplishments. We may be clever at hiding our true selves from each other but the root cause of the shame is still the same.

The fallout from sin causes us to use one another instead of loving one another. Sin ruined and continues to devastate beautiful love relationships that God intended for us to enjoy from the beginning. Adam and Eve's story ended with banishment from the garden and the world's first sinners gave birth to the world's first murderer. However, there is hope. The bad news is that there is really nothing we can do about the problem of sin. The good news is that God can and did do something to get rid of sin and its consequences. As Christians, we believe that the punishment for Adam and Eve's sin was nailed to the cross. Jesus paid the price for our sins. "But God proves his love for us in that while we still were sinners Christ died for us" (Romans 5:8).

What God did through Jesus affords us the opportunity to go back to the beginning, to go back to the way things were meant to be. Our lives, our relationships, our world has been redeemed by Jesus' death and resurrection.

Adam and Eve never returned to the garden but, in a sense, we can. We can go back to the way God intended with the assistance of the Holy Spirit. Adam and Eve missed out on all that God had in store for them. We still have a choice to make. Will we love and give ourselves totally, freely, faithfully, and fruitfully to each other and to God?

It's as true today as it was in the garden; it's not good for man to be alone. We are created to be in a community of persons. Man and woman, created in the image of God, are in a sense complete when they give themselves to each other as God gives himself to us.

PRAYER

Heavenly Father, you created us to be in unity with you and each other. Heal our brokenness in whatever form it takes. Guard us from the deception of Satan and the allure of evil which brings death. Save us from our own selfishness. Let our love for each other reflect the love you have for each of us. May our love be fruitful and faithful as we strive to love as completely as you love. Mary, Mother of God, be our protector against the lies of the evil one and bring our needs to your Son who alone can make all things new. Amen.

QUOTE

"God is not solitude, but perfect communion. For this reason the human person, the image of God, realizes himself or herself in love, which is a sincere gift of self."

—*Pope Benedict XVI*[1]

REFLECTION QUESTIONS

Describe a few of the healthy relationships you have experienced. What made them work?

Have you ever felt that you were alone or isolated from others? Was it a difficult time? What, if any, good came from it?

Have you encountered the excitement of Adam in being in a relationship with another who understood you and completed you? What words describe that relationship?

When sin enters the relationship things go south quickly. Have you ever experienced the heartache of a broken relationship?

With sin came death. With forgiveness comes hope. Have you experienced a reconciliation that restored a broken relationship? How was it made right?

LOVE CONNECTION
Reach out to someone who has been helpful to you and let them know you are thinking about them.

chapter two

ABRAHAM AND SARAH
TRUSTING THE ONE YOU LOVE

Rarely, if ever, does life turn out as we plan. Marriage, for example, with its twists and turns, can lead us down an unexpected path. That new home, the job promotion, and even the welcoming of children can be postponed due to changing circumstances. It all comes down to God's timing, but the waiting can be brutal on a couple. Expectations change as life moves along. Abraham and Sarah are perfect examples of the need to trust in God along the crooked path of life.

We first come upon this couple early in the book of Genesis. We find a man named Abram, son of Terah, and his wife, Sarai. Both Abram and Sarai would later have their names changed by God to Abraham and Sarah, respectively. We are given little information about Sarah, only that she was without child. However, Abraham and Sarah form one of the most formidable husband-and-wife teams in the Bible. Together they are mentioned over three hundred times in both the Old and New Testaments. Our spiritual heritage can be traced to the covenant God made with Abraham and the promises fulfilled in Sarah. From these humble introductions we see this couple used by God in powerful ways.

Most likely Abraham and Sarah had reasonable expectations of a simple life filled with children to love. However, this was not what God had planned for this couple. As we are told in Genesis, God wanted more from Abraham and Sarah—total trust and faith. "Now the LORD said to Abram, 'Go from your country and your kindred and your father's house to the land that I will show you. I will make of you a great nation, and I will bless you, and make your name great, so that you will be a blessing'" (Genesis 12:1–2).

The couple's willingness to follow the Lord reveals their deep faith both in God and in one another. It's hard to imagine how most of us would respond if our spouse announced that we should leave everything we know and move to an unknown land. But Sarah trusted Abraham and did as God commanded. We can suppose that this was not a one-time action for Abraham and Sarah, but rather the habit of a lifetime centered on God.

God told Abraham to leave his country, his family, and his father's house, but not his wife. There was a partnership implied in God's call. In the New Testament Sarah is noted for two things: her faith in God (Hebrews 11:11) and her submission to her husband (1 Peter 3:5–6). This "submission" is not a quality of weakness, but rather of strength. She trusted that God, who brought her and Abraham together, was working through her husband to accomplish good. Sarah's self-sacrificing love and desire to put God's will before her own plays a key role in salvation history.

Sarah's mission in life was to work with her husband to fulfill God's purposes. This mission was not born of weakness, but of fortitude and prudence. As we first read of Abraham and Sarah we are drawn to their faith in God and to their mutual love of one another. The journey they started together in marriage was going to end together.

Sarah trusted Abraham implicitly, even when he advised her to lie about their relationship.

> When he was about to enter Egypt, he said to his wife Sarai, "I know well that you are a woman beautiful in appearance; and when the Egyptians see you, they will say, 'This is his wife'; then they will kill me, but they will let you live. Say you are my sister, so that it may go well with me because of you, and that my life may be spared on your account." (Genesis 12:11–13)

Sarah does not have an obligation to obey a request that clearly goes against the will of God, but her obedience reveals her trust in Abraham and in God. She knew that if Abraham were to become the father of a great nation, he would have to live.

While Abraham was a man of great faith, he was human, which brings him closer to us. His humanity was revealed when he advised Sarah to lie. He compromised his wife to protect himself. Abraham failed Sarah miserably in this episode of their life but she didn't abandon him, and neither does God.

One of God's promises to Abraham was that he would father many descendants. How could this be when Abraham had no children? Sarah devised a plan that was based, one could suppose, on love, yet was a flawed, human solution to a divine problem. Sarah offered her slave girl, Hagar, to bear a child for Abraham. While her intention was noble, her lack of faith in God was evident. Of course Abraham could have rejected Sarah's offer, but he did not. Hagar bore a son, Ishmael, and trouble ensued. Regardless of their failings, God remained faithful to his covenant with Abraham.

> God said to Abraham, "As for Sarai your wife, you shall not call her Sarai, but Sarah shall be her name. I will bless her, and moreover I will give you a son by her. I will bless her, and she shall give rise to nations; kings of peoples shall come from her."

> Then Abraham fell on his face and laughed, and said to himself,
> "Can a child be born to a man who is a hundred years old? Can
> Sarah, who is ninety years old, bear a child?" And Abraham
> said to God, "O that Ishmael might live in your sight!" God
> said, "No, but your wife Sarah shall bear you a son, and you
> shall name him Isaac. I will establish my covenant with him as
> an everlasting covenant for his offspring after him." (Genesis
> 17:15–19)

Next it was Sarah's turn to hear God's message on the fulfillment
of his promises. "Is anything too wonderful for the Lord? At the
set time I will return to you, in due season, and Sarah shall have
a son" (Genesis 18:14). While Sarah was beyond the normal
childbearing age, she trusted in God and soon conceived a child.

God continued to challenge the couple as he told Abraham to
humbly trust his wife. "But God said to Abraham, 'Do not be dis-
tressed because of the boy and because of your slave woman;
whatever Sarah says to you, do as she tells you, for it is through
Isaac that offspring shall be named for you'" (Genesis 21:12).
God used Sarah to correct her husband, to offer him insight and
advice. Just as it was difficult for Abraham, it is often difficult for
men today to trust their wives in matters of faith and discernment.
How often do we fail to see our spouses as instruments of God's
wisdom?

Abraham's trust paid off when God fulfilled his promise and
Sarah gave birth to a son. But the couple's greatest test was yet to
come. In one of the most unusual scenes in the Bible, God asks
Abraham to sacrifice his son, Isaac. After the promise, after the
years of waiting, God commanded Abraham to kill his child. "He
said, 'Take your son, your only son Isaac, whom you love, and go
to the land of Moriah, and offer him there as a burnt-offering on
one of the mountains that I shall show you'" (Genesis 22:2).

While Sarah is not mentioned by name in the text, we can reasonably assume she knew what was going on. The wood, the knife, and the look of sheer agony on her husband's face as he left with Isaac must have struck fear into her heart. I can imagine her looking through the opening of the tent as they disappeared up Mt. Moriah. Did Abraham reveal to her what God had asked? Was the news too difficult for Abraham to deliver? While Scripture gives us little information on Sarah, it again reveals her trust in her husband and in her Lord.

As the story goes, God stops Abraham from sacrificing his only son. We then learn of Sarah's death and burial in a place of honor.

Rarely does life turn out as we plan. Yet Abraham and Sarah, together as a couple, showed love for God and each other through mutual submission. Despite their failures, God remained faithful. In the end love prevailed and a nation was born.

PRAYER

Lord God, be close to me and to my loved ones when life doesn't turn out as we planned. Echo in our hearts at the right moment when life is most unpredictable that you are never unfaithful and will never leave us. Give us the grace to see God working through our spouse and our loved ones and that we need each other for strength and support along the way. Forgive us when we forget you and out of fear and lack of faith take matters into our own hands. Bring us back to you and help us to remain faithful in all things great and small. Amen.

QUOTE

"We can't have full knowledge all at once. We must start by believing; then afterwards we may be led on to master the evidence for ourselves."

—*Saint Thomas Aquinas*[2]

REFLECTION QUESTIONS

Think of a time when you felt that God called you to do the unexpected. What was the outcome? Did you grow from the experience?

Can you think of a time when God spoke to you through another, be it a spouse or another human being? What convinced you that it was God speaking through that person?

Abraham and Sarah felt God calling them to a "foreign land." Are there any "foreign lands" in your life that God may be calling you to, such as stepping out into a new ministry or reaching out to a friend to invite them to a Christian event?

How can you include your spouse and family in discerning God's will for your marriage, family, and calling in life?

LOVE CONNECTION

Be attentive to the Holy Spirit moving in the life of your spouse and family and affirm them in your speech and actions.

chapter three

REBEKAH AND ISAAC
A MARRIAGE ORDAINED BY GOD

The last time we encountered Isaac in the Scriptures his father, Abraham, had him carry wood up Mt. Moriah and then laid him on the altar to be sacrificed. But God intervened! We will see God intervening in Isaac's life again, for just as God had a plan for Abraham and Sarah, so, too, did he have a plan for Isaac and Rebekah. Their marriage was ordained by God.

Chapter twenty-four of the book of Genesis describes Abraham as an old man, now widowed, and thinking about his son's future. He makes plans for his oldest servant to find a wife for his son in his native land, which is different from the place he is currently living. The oldest servant makes an oath and is on his way, following the command of Abraham. We see something of the servant's character as he approaches a well and prays for guidance. He asks God to guide him through fortunate circumstances and reveal his will in a clear way. He prays, "Let the girl to whom I shall say, 'Please offer your jar that I may drink,' and who shall say, 'Drink, and I will water your camels'—let her be the one whom you have appointed for your servant Isaac. By this I shall know that you have shown steadfast love to my master" (Genesis 24:14).

The servant doesn't make up the rules as he goes along, but rather makes it clear before he sets out on his journey the woman for whom he is searching. The servant asked for a sign that was extraordinary, but not impossible. The action of the woman revealed something about her character and the depth of her interior beauty. One might be tempted to pray for the "best looking gal in the valley," but the servant did just the opposite. He sought a woman who could express her love through her kindness, service, and generosity toward strangers.

As the servant made many trips to the well, he prayed for Isaac's mate. Before he had finished praying "...have shown steadfast love to my master..." there she stood: Rebekah! God knows the desires of our heart and delights in providing for our needs when they are in line with his will, even before the words escape our lips. While the servant didn't know his prayer was answered immediately, time would tell who had arranged this meeting.

Rebekah is the only woman in the Old Testament whose birth is recorded in Scripture, which should alert us to her significance in salvation history. She is honored for her faith and trust in God, who speaks directly to her.

Rebekah is beautiful and the servant runs to introduce himself to her. How often do we pray and then wait for someone else to begin the conversation, or for the phone to ring? In this case, the servant is not afraid to go out to meet her. He has prayed and won't be delayed because prayer is no replacement for action. She quickly gives the servant a drink of water and then proceeds to water the camels. Her hospitality to the stranger opens the door for further dialogue and service. Rebekah had a servant's heart.

Abraham's servant places the traditional and costly adornments on Rebekah, a ring and bracelets, and then inquires as to who she is. She tells him of her father and the servant's first actions are to bow down and to worship God. "Blessed be the LORD, the God of my master Abraham, who has not forsaken his steadfast love and his faithfulness towards my master. As for me, the LORD has led me on the way to the house of my master's kin" (Genesis 24:27). His remark that "the Lord has led me" can also be translated that, "the Lord has guided my steps." It was the servant who was walking and taking action, but it was God who was leading the way.

After enjoying the hospitality of Rebekah's family, the servant enjoins her to go with him back to meet Isaac. The brothers and mother want her to delay for a while, maybe up to ten days. This is a natural reaction for most people when encountering a new and perhaps frightening situation. We are convinced that it is God's will but let's just wait a little bit more. The family lays the decision at Rebekah's feet and she replies with firmness and confidence. "They said, 'We will call the girl, and ask her.' And they called Rebekah, and said to her, 'Will you go with this man?' She said, 'I will'" (Genesis 24:57–58).

What a remarkable step of faith for Rebekah! She would leave her home and family and travel hundreds of miles on camelback with an unfamiliar person, to marry a man she had never met. It was her faith in God's providence that enabled her to say, "I will."

As the caravan draws closer we meet Isaac, who is out walking in the desert. What thoughts ran through his head as he saw the dust rise on the horizon? What expectations did he have? Was he praying on his walk? Did the long time between the departure of the servant and his arrival cause him to question God? Did he reflect on the faith of his father who had also waited a long time for God's promise to be fulfilled?

After hearing the story from the servant about how he found Rebekah, he took her into his tent and made her his wife. The last commentary we have from this passage is that, "…he loved her."

In reflecting on how Isaac gave himself to Rebekah we are reminded of how God is the source of all love as he gives Isaac the gift of a wife. It is a story of God's providential care for those who seek his will for their lives in all things.

How often do we relegate to God only those things in which we feel he should have a say, yet exclude him from the ordinary things in life? How often do we make decisions and then ask for God's blessing, when what we really need is God's guidance?

What is not mentioned in the story is Isaac's mind-set. We last left him on a pile of wood about to be sacrificed when God told Abraham to stop. His father was obedient to God, for he held nothing back, surrendering totally. Being raised by a man of such great faith undoubtedly had a profound influence on Isaac.

Did Isaac walk continually at night, in silence, waiting for God's timing? Do we walk in darkness, as well, seeking God's will and provision in our lives? There is the temptation to take matters into our own hands apart from the will of God and we fail to receive all that God has planned for us. This story begins in a tent with two people totally giving themselves to each other in love after totally giving themselves to God who ordained their marriage.

PRAYER

God of surprises! Surprise us with your presence, your love, and provision for all the needs of our lives. We ask you, the Giver of all good things, for the strength to move forward with our lives, especially during times of trial and anxiety. Let our prayers reflect the desires of our hearts and may we never hold anything back from you. Heal our wounds and self-doubt and give us the determination and confidence of Rebekah who acted decisively when she believed God's will was being done. Amen.

QUOTE

"Have no fear of moving into the unknown. Simply step out fearlessly knowing that I am with you, therefore no harm can befall you; all is very, very well. Do this in complete faith and confidence."

—*Pope John Paul II*[3]

REFLECTION QUESTIONS

Often God works through others to accomplish his will. Can you think of a person whom God has worked through in your life? Did you recognize that God's "hand" was on the person at the time?

Before the servant finished praying, Rebekah was in sight. Are you more optimistic or pessimistic about having God answer your prayer? How does this story change or reinforce your outlook?

The servant prayed and then acted. Do you do the same or is your prayer life or action lacking?

Prayer preceded action. Have you ever reversed the order and acted and then hoped God was on your side? How can having a consistent prayer routine help put your priorities in order? Do you set time aside to pray? What's preventing you?

LOVE CONNECTION

Take time to notice those who are serving today, be they at home, work, school, or in your family and let them know you appreciate their service.

chapter four

JACOB AND RACHEL
THE KISS

"Then Jacob kissed Rachel, and wept aloud."

Fireworks sparked when Jacob and Rachel first met! A glance at her beauty swept him off of his feet and then... the kiss. So powerful was this kiss that the Bible records that Jacob, "...wept aloud." It is not customary for men of this culture to show such a public display of emotion, so we know that this must have been some kiss! This is the first biblical account of a romantic kiss. The story of Rachel and Jacob doesn't end there, but it's worth considering what comes immediately before.

Jacob set out on a journey to the land that his father, Isaac, had directed him in search of a wife. He encounters God in a very powerful dream and God vows to be with him, protect him, and never leave him until he has fulfilled his promises. Jacob renames the place "Bethel" and marks it with a memorial stone.

Jacob arrives in Haran and comes upon a well with three flocks of sheep surrounding it. During this time wells were dug into the ground and a stone was placed directly on top of the opening to prevent both people and animals from falling in. After making some inquiries as to whether the shepherds at the well knew of his family living in the region, he then asked why they had not watered their sheep. They responded that they had to wait for the fourth shepherd to arrive so they can move the stone off the well. Then along comes Rachel with her father's flock. We can imagine Jacob's gaze as he sees Rachel for the first time. Wham! Love at first sight! Rachel's beauty stirs an emotional response in Jacob that may not be what we would expect. Rather than experiencing a primarily sexual desire, Jacob desired to serve this woman.

Jacob does not run up, grab her, and kiss her passionately. First he moves the stone, waters the sheep and, only after serving her, he kisses her. Her response is also revealing; she runs as quickly as possible to tell her father. She will not bring dishonor to her father and her people with this kiss without her father's knowledge. Rachel, whose name literally means *ewe*, reflects the purity and innocence of a lamb. Her name reflects her character.

The kiss is a common form of greeting among men in Middle Eastern cultures. Given on the cheek, the forehead, the beard, or the hands, this outward sign of welcome and brotherhood was expected to be given to relatives, while paying homage in friendship and love. In the New Testament Saint Paul encourages the Thessalonians to, "Greet all the brothers and sisters with a holy kiss" (1 Thessalonians 5:26). In Luke 7:38 we read about a "sinful" woman who goes to Jesus' feet and kisses them. And perhaps the most famous kiss of all is the kiss of betrayal by Judas in Luke 22:47–48. However, for Jacob and Rachel, the kiss is a sign of deep affection. These first things, this mutual respect at their first meeting bode well; they have a true passion for one another. But, does all that starts well end well?

As the story moves on we read of Rachel's father, Laban, who had an older daughter called Leah. Jacob asks for Rachel to be given in marriage in return for seven years of service to him. Because Jacob had no money or possessions to give Laban, his work was all he had to offer. Seven years of service! Wow, times were certainly different back then. However, when in love, any sacrifice seems worth it. His response to the seven years of service encapsulates perhaps the most beautiful sentiment of a man to a woman, "So Jacob served seven years for Rachel, yet they seemed to him but a few days because of his love for her" (Genesis 29:20).

Seven years is a long time to wait. While her physical beauty was undeniable, Jacob surely came to learn of Rachel's good and bad qualities during this time period. The times ahead would present some challenges, but this engagement period would provide them with the maturing love they would need to see it through. Through his waiting, Jacob is communicating that he is willing to sacrifice for her. If it is love, it will stand the test of time.

As the seven years come to an end and the big day is upon them, Jacob suffers an intolerable blow. Laban switches daughters! Jacob consummates his marriage with a veiled Leah instead of Rachel! What a rotten thing to do—to put it mildly. Jacob is furious. Laban defends his decision by explaining that it is customary that the older daughter marry first. I can't imagine that Leah was not in on the scheme as well. What an awful way to start a marriage. The long-term consequences for a marriage built on dishonesty and deceit are always painful and agonizing.

After the bridal week is over and the wedding festivities conclude, Laban changes his mind again and agrees to allow Jacob to marry Rachel—if Jacob agrees to work for seven more years without pay. We hear the words of God in the book of Genesis echo in the background of this text, for his will is one man for one woman. Yet this patriarch enters into a bigamous relationship.

What were his alternatives? Should he have stayed married to Leah? He could have rejected her on their wedding night. He could have learned to love and serve her. After all, Jacob's father was forced to accept the consequences of Jacob's deceit in impersonating his brother Esau. A tall order, but he could have accepted this as God's will for his life.

Rachel, seeing that Leah bear Jacob children, becomes furious and envious and demands of Jacob, "Give me children or I shall die!" Rachel's demeanor was changing, and on a human level, who can blame her? Rachel is witnessing her husband having relations with her sister and she's bearing children for him left and right. Rachel became dissatisfied while Jacob became angry. Discontentment enters.

In a move that seems quite bizarre to our cultural norms, Rachel gave her handmaid Bilhah to Jacob so that he could have a son by her, and she conceived twice. In that culture and time period, the children of that union would be considered Rachel's children. Later, in Genesis 30:14–15, we read that she allows Leah to sleep with Jacob in return for a few mandrakes! The union that God brought together was turning into a circus.

While Rachel's jealousy is evident and her attitude has changed, only once does Scripture reveal that Jacob became angry with her. Jacob never loved Rachel any less. His protective love of her never diminished throughout their remaining years together. We read of Jacob near the end of his life in Genesis 48:7 blessing his sons and remarking that, "I came from Paddan, Rachel died, to my sorrow..." She is buried on the road leading from Bethlehem to Jerusalem.

This love story begins with service and a kiss. Rachel's and Jacob's lives together take some unexpected twists and turns, but through their love and suffering a nation will be born. Jacob's sons will form the twelve tribes of Israel and will bear fruit far beyond what he and Rachel can imagine.

PRAYER

God of Abraham, Isaac, and Jacob, guide us in our choice for a spouse and for the spouses of our children. Give us the grace to love and to serve our spouse and may our love for you overflow into every relationship we encounter. May the sacrifices for our loved ones be done with zeal and joy and remind us that in loving each other we are loving you. Grant that others will be attracted to us not only by outward appearance but by a faith, hope, love, and joy that comes from God alone. Amen.

QUOTE

"Marriage based on exclusive and definitive love becomes the icon of the relationship between God and his people and vice versa. God's way of loving becomes the measure of human love."

—*Pope Benedict XVI*[4]

REFLECTION QUESTIONS

In our culture what personal qualities or characteristics are highlighted as being important? Are these qualities the basis for a lasting relationship?

Who has loved you by serving you? Think back to your childhood and teenage years. Are there some people who helped you become the person you are through their love for you as expressed through service?

Out of the pain and suffering of Jacob and Rachel a nation is born. Can you reflect on a time in your life when something good came out of pain and suffering? Was it something tangible or perhaps a changed perspective?

What may be some cultural norms that we accept today that are opposed to the will of God as expressed in his Word or in the teaching of your faith community?

LOVE CONNECTION

Intentionally give of yourself today in some small, anonymous way and don't count the cost.

chapter five

JOSEPH AND HIS BROTHERS
RADICAL RECONCILIATION

The ability to forgive is one of the qualities that come right from the heart of God. God's merciful love enables us to forgive others. Mother Teresa said that it, "takes great love to forgive but even greater humility to ask for forgiveness." This is probably the reason why there is so much anger, jealousy, hatred, war, and division in our world...not to mention all the medication for upset stomachs and ulcers!

Often I think that the virtue of forgiveness is one that Jesus and his followers have perfected, if not all together invented. But before Jesus, before Isaiah, before King David, and before Elijah, we come to one of the holiest men of the Bible: Joseph. If any person had the right to get his "pound of flesh," it was this righteous man. His response to the violent maltreatment, false accusations, and abuse he received is a challenge for all who claim to follow God.

"I am Joseph your brother..."

If you are not familiar with the story of Joseph and his brothers in Genesis chapters 37 to 50, you may think those words would be music to his brothers' ears. "Ah, finally my brother, one whom I trust, one whom we can share a meal with and tell the same old family stories again! My brother is here, now I am finally at home." Well, think again. Joseph, son of Jacob, reveals himself to his brothers who had every right to be terrified.

A brief account of the story Joseph begins with his parents, Jacob and Rachel. He was his father's eleventh son. As a boy, Joseph received an elegant coat from his father. He also dreamed that the sun, moon, and eleven stars bowed down before him, which he interpreted to mean that one day Joseph's family members would bow down before him. His brothers became angry at hearing this, sold the boy as a slave to a band of Ishmaelites who brought him to Egypt, and bloodied his coat to make their father believe Joseph was dead. In Egypt, Joseph rose to a position of influence, but was imprisoned on false charges of making advances on his master's wife. After interpreting Pharaoh's dreams which foretold famine, he was released and given the responsibility of managing Egypt's food supply. When famine struck, Joseph's brothers came to Egypt in search of food. At first Joseph disguised his identity, held one of his brothers hostage, and demanded that the rest bring their youngest brother, Benjamin, to Egypt. When they returned, Joseph revealed his identity and brought his entire family to live in Egypt.

> Then Joseph said to his brothers, "Come closer to me." And they came closer. He said, "I am your brother Joseph, whom you sold into Egypt. And now do not be distressed, or angry with yourselves, because you sold me here; for God sent me before you to preserve life. For the famine has been in the land these two years; and there are five more years in which there will be neither plowing nor harvest. God sent me before you to preserve for you a remnant on earth, and to keep alive for you many survivors. So it was not you who sent me here, but God; he has made me a father to Pharaoh, and lord of all his house and ruler over all the land of Egypt." (Genesis 45:4–8)

What enabled Joseph to speak these words to his brothers? Three times Joseph mentions that it was God, not his brothers, who really sent him to Egypt. Joseph received everything from the hand of God, including suffering, false accusations, and humiliation. Because of his belief in God, Joseph was able to do something that most of us cannot: He changed his perspective on his life. We judge things from our limited, imperfect, human point of view and often make incorrect judgments. Joseph, who didn't protest verbally during the injustices forced upon him, considered his life from God's perspective. This made him able to forgive and to love those who hurt him.

Joseph's love for his brothers was sincere; it was not just hollow words of forgiveness. He states beautifully, "I will provide for you there—since there are five more years of famine to come—so that you and your household, and all that you have, will not come to poverty" (Genesis 45:11). "And he kissed all his brothers and wept upon them; and after that his brothers talked with him" (Genesis 45:15).

Joseph continues to be a model of complete and total surrender to God. The witness of his life speaks volumes. There was no "eye for an eye" or "tooth for a tooth" with Joseph. Through it all he is a man of faith and love, as expressed through forgiveness, reconciliation, and provision.

PRAYER

Shepherd of Israel, teach us to forgive and to reconcile like Joseph. Allow us the grace to accept all of life's trials from your hands. Heal us from wounds caused by others and forgive us for the times we have wounded others by our words, conduct, and neglect. We bring our whole self to you and ask that you eliminate all envy, jealousy, and injustice and all the root causes that lead us away from you and others. Remind us often that you are in control and have a purpose for everything that occurs in our lives. Amen.

QUOTE

"No one likes being trapped. Fear takes over and darkness over-shadows you. It is how victims of bullying constantly feel. We become frightened not only of the bully but of standing up for ourselves. We hide the light within ourselves that can overcome the darkness. When Joseph was in prison, he felt that darkness. Joseph's brothers sold him into slavery. He was falsely accused and sent to prison. Joseph suffered injustice, but allowed God to use him as a vessel to interpret dreams. He forgave his brothers and Potiphar by his actions. He let God work through him to make the best of his situation. We must become vessels of God's light. While bullying left its scars, it left me compassion. I value the love of my friends. There is always a light in the darkness. Can we be willing to spread God's guiding light where our fear lies most?"

—*Elizabeth Tartaglia* (in formation with the
Sisters of Christian Charity)[5]

REFLECTION QUESTIONS

Which do you find easier: to forgive or to ask forgiveness?

Only when Joseph was older did he say that it was really God who brought him to Egypt. Have you ever had a change of perspective on a difficult experience after the passage of time?

When we forgive we set a captive free and we realize that we were the captive! Have you ever experienced the freedom that forgiveness brings either with God or with others?

Have you ever been in a position to offer forgiveness like Joseph? Was it difficult? Were there strings attached?

Are there any areas in your life that you need to "get right with God" or with others? What is your next course of action?

LOVE CONNECTION
Spend some time examining your conscience and ask for the grace to forgive and the fortitude and humility to ask for forgiveness.

chapter six

ABIGAIL AND DAVID
BRAINS, BEAUTY, AND LOVE

Abigail is one of the most respected and acclaimed women in all of Judaism. Her brains, beauty, and prophetic voice literally stopped David, the future king of Israel, in his tracks. Her quick thinking and action impressed David and helped him to become the God-fearing leader that he was called to be. Abigail saw in David what he failed to see in himself. This would prove the most powerful lesson he would learn. David would not be able to reign as king until he had learned to let God reign in his own life. This lesson came through Abigail's straightforward but gentle love at a crucial point in David's young life.

In the first book of Samuel we read, "Now the name of the man was Nabal, and the name of his wife Abigail. The woman was clever and beautiful, but the man was surly and mean; he was a Calebite" (1 Samuel 25:3). The name *Abigail* means, "joy of my father" so it is safe to assume that her father adored her and treated her well. However, when we come across Abigail in the Bible she is married to an awful man named Nabal whose name means "fool," and who came to be associated with failure.

How or why she ended up in this relationship is unknown, but her profound insight and quick thinking would come to be known the world over.

As the story unfolds, David sends ten of his young men over to Nabal, who lives in Carmel and instructs them to,

> Go up to Carmel, and go to Nabal, and greet him in my name. Thus you shall salute him: "Peace be to you, and peace be to your house, and peace be to all that you have. I hear that you have shearers; now your shepherds have been with us, and we did them no harm, and they missed nothing, all the time they were in Carmel. Ask your young men, and they will tell you. Therefore let my young men find favor in your sight; for we have come on a feast day. Please give whatever you have at hand to your servants and to your son David." (1 Samuel 25:5–8)

Nabal's response is not what David expected. He outright refuses David and his men any hospitality in the way of food or drink. David is outraged and in his anger grabs his sword with the plan to shed the blood of Nabal and his family. In response to David's actions, Abigail quickly, "took two hundred loaves, two skins of wine, five sheep ready dressed, five measures of parched grain, one hundred clusters of raisins, and two hundred cakes of figs. She loaded them on donkeys and said to her young men, 'Go on ahead of me; I am coming after you'"(1 Samuel 25:18–19). She did this without informing her husband.

As David and his men rode toward Carmel to destroy Nabal and his family, his rage intensified. His kindness had been repaid with evil and so he was about to take revenge—until he met Abigail. She dismounted from her donkey and lay prostrate in front of him and did him homage. She fell at his feet, addresses him as "My Lord," and asked that the blame due Nabal fall to her. She boldly asked permission to speak, begged him to listen, and in humility addressed herself as "handmaid." What happens next is remarkable, for Abigail corrected David in such a way that he is open to the rebuke. We shall see God using the prophet Nathan later on in David's life to admonish him by way of a parable, but here, a woman confronts David and informs him that his way is not God's way.

> Now then, my lord, as the Lord lives, and as you yourself live, since the Lord has restrained you from blood-guilt and from taking vengeance with your own hand, now let your enemies and those who seek to do evil to my lord be like Nabal. And now let this present that your servant has brought to my lord be given to the young men who follow my lord. Please forgive the trespass of your servant; for the Lord will certainly make my lord a sure house, because my lord is fighting the battles of the Lord; and evil shall not be found in you as long as you live. (1 Samuel 25:26–28)

In effect, Abigail tells David that he is wrong, and that what he is doing is evil. She informs him that when he becomes king, this act of revenge will not be forgotten. Abigail beautifully states that, "the life of my lord shall be bound in the bundle of the living under the care of the LORD your God" (1 Samuel 25:29).

Abigail courageously communicates to David that the battle he is fighting is God's battle, and the life that he is living is God's life. She advises him to trust that God will care for him and defend him. That is quite a strong reproach coming from an unfamiliar woman to a man who is soon to be king of Israel. And while the rebuke is forceful, Abigail is gentle as a dove as she addresses him as "lord" and bows before him. Twice she asks for forgiveness for saying what she says. It was her husband who sinned, yet she is interceding for him and protecting David from himself. She does not scold him or raise her voice, but speaks out of tenderness and compassion. It wasn't a desire to seek her own will, but rather, to see David become the king that God intended him to be.

David, to his credit, listened and recognized the voice of God coming through Abigail and he received it as such. David's first words of response point toward God, for Abigail had turned his eyes away from Nabal and his own desire for revenge and back to the Lord.

> "Blessed be the LORD, the God of Israel, who sent you to meet me today! Blessed be your good sense, and blessed be you, who have kept me today from blood-guilt and from avenging myself by my own hand! For as surely as the Lord the God of Israel lives, who has restrained me from hurting you, unless you had hurried and come to meet me, truly by morning there would not have been left to Nabal as much as one male." Then David received from her hand what she had brought him; he said to her, "Go up to your house in peace; see, I have heeded your voice, and I have granted your petition." (1 Samuel 25:32–35)

Abigail turned David to the Lord and his praise of her is not for her beauty or her intelligence, but rather for her discernment and understanding of God's ways. Soon after, Nabal, upon hearing what his wife had done, was struck to the core in shock and died ten days later. David hears the news and rejoices. He proposes marriage to Abigail and she accepts.

Abigail, who changed the heart of the future king by reminding him of God's ways, was indeed the joy of her heavenly Father.

PRAYER

Lord God, you saved David from himself through your servant Abigail. Send people into our lives to correct us on our way when through our own foolishness, ignorance, and pride we stray from you. May the gentleness and honesty of Abigail be our model in fraternal correction and may our thoughts and hearts always be focused on you. Amen.

QUOTE

"What strikes me most about the beautiful story of Abigail and David is the willingness of both to step out of their comfort zones and do what they knew to be righteous. How terrifying that must have been for Abigail to reprimand the future king of Israel. She had to have known the risks that her actions carried. But she put her fears aside and did what she knew to be right. And David, in turn, allowed himself to be open to hear Abigail's words. How easy it would have been for him to silence this woman who dared cross him. How many opportunities in life pass us by simply because we do not allow ourselves to be open: to act, to speak, to listen? How many friends have we lost, how many loved ones have we hurt, how many lives have we failed to touch, all because our hearts and minds were closed? Thankfully, Abigail and David did not allow the cultural norms of the time to stop them from following their hearts. What a beautiful partnership they would build, and what a beautiful example for us they became."

—*Amber Dolle*[6]

REFLECTION QUESTIONS

Do you feel that your battles are God's as well? Do you trust that God will take care of your needs?

Is there anyone in your life that you have to remind of God's ways? What is the potential danger if the correction is not done gently and is not received well?

Put yourself in Abigail's shoes for a minute. Would it have been difficult for you to confront David, the future king, as Abigail did? Has there ever been a time when you had to convince someone to change their course of action as Abigail convinced David?

LOVE CONNECTION

In humility, ask God to send someone your way that may gently correct you and remind you of God.

chapter seven

DAVID AND JONATHAN
THE BOND OF BROTHERS

In the pages of 1 Samuel and 2 Samuel we read about two men, David and Jonathan, whose friendship and love for one another is united in God.

> When David had finished speaking to Saul, the soul of Jonathan was bound to the soul of David, and Jonathan loved him as his own soul. Saul took him that day and would not let him return to his father's house. Then Jonathan made a covenant with David, because he loved him as his own soul. Jonathan stripped himself of the robe that he was wearing, and gave it to David, and his armor, and even his sword and his bow and his belt. (1 Samuel 18:1–4)

Nothing brings people together more than a battle. The bonding that takes place while waging war, fighting a fire, or going against a common opponent is unique. Only those who have experienced the struggle fully understand the solidarity and camaraderie that it brings. Ask any World War II or Vietnam veteran, or any New York City firefighter or police officer who lost a buddy on September 11, and they will freely tell you of their love for their fallen comrade. Ask any athlete about a game that was down to the wire and they can instantly return to that moment in time: the inning and the pitch, the down and yardage, the seconds ticking away on the clock. Soldiers and athletes often form bonds of love that last a lifetime. It's a love borne out of a shared experience. The thrill of victory and the agony of defeat unite us to moments in our lives like nothing else can.

David and Jonathan were two men connected as brothers, for they were brothers-in-arms during war. Jonathan was King Saul's eldest son, the heir apparent to the throne, a man intensely loyal to his father. He also held a deep loyalty to David, the young warrior who had just killed Goliath. As the story proceeds, it is evident that the tension intensifies as Jonathan is caught between two loyalties. He should have been the next king, but David had already been anointed king secretly by Samuel in Bethlehem. Jonathan knew that it was only a matter of time before David would take his place on the throne.

While Jonathan's loyalty to David was true and sincere, he was also loyal to his father. The story of Jonathan's friendship with David develops out of this tension and we read that Jonathan "cast his lot" with David. No doubt Jonathan and David thought alike; they were both warriors who looked at life through the same lens. Jonathan's belief in God can be found in his own words, "Come, let us go over to the garrison of these uncircumcised; it may be that the LORD will act for us; for nothing can hinder the LORD from saving by many or by few" (1 Samuel 14:6). In other words, Jonathan knew that if the Lord was with him the plan would succeed, despite his own strength or numbers.

David felt the same about the Lord as he is described as a man "after God's own heart" (see 1 Samuel 13:14). As the most famous author of Psalms, David reveals his trust in the Lord beautifully and poetically. While David and Jonathan were not related, they shared a faith in God, and such a bond runs deeper than blood.

As David is explaining to Saul his victory over Goliath, Jonathan's heart was bound to the heart of David, and he made a covenant with him. This is often where the bond of friendship begins for us as well. We are attracted to people who believe like us, are involved in the same activities, find the same things humorous, and share our perspective on life. This initial attraction is the "beginning of a beautiful friendship" as Humphrey Bogart put it in the movie *Casablanca*. For many people the initial relationship never gets any deeper, there is no real commitment to the other, and no shared experiences. However, Jonathan did take his friendship to the next level.

In an expression of his friendship and love, Jonathan offers a pledge, a covenant, to David. Biblical covenants—relationships based upon mutual commitment that last until death—normally involved a pledge. This is what we see Jonathan doing here by pledging himself to David. This act was symbolized in the giving of his garment to David. He did not totally strip himself of all clothing, but rather took off "the robe that he was wearing, and gave it to David, and his armor, and even his sword and his bow and his belt" (1 Samuel 18:4). To receive the robe of a member of a royal family, such as Jonathan, was an extreme honor.

Presenting David with his armor, sword, bow, and belt also symbolized his submission to God as he recognizes David, not his father, as the Lord's anointed. He gives totally of himself, which is the essence of friendship and love. Jesus will say one thousand years later that, "No one has greater love than this, to lay down one's life for one's friends" (John 15:13). Jonathan is truly laying down his life for his friend.

The Hebrew word for love used in this text, *ahava*, describes the love between two sexual partners less than twenty percent of the time. Usually the word describes the love between friends, between God and man, and the relationship between God and his creation.

After defeating the Amalekites in a battle, David abruptly learns of the death of both Saul and Jonathan. David composes a song as a way of expressing his grief and love for his fallen comrade and orders the people of Judah to learn the tribute in order to honor the man:

> I am distressed for you, my brother Jonathan;
> greatly beloved were you to me;
> your love to me was wonderful,
> passing the love of women.
> How the mighty have fallen,
> and the weapons of war perished! (2 Samuel 1:23–27)

Such is the strength of David's love for his brother-in-arms.

PRAYER

Heavenly Father, thank you for the friends and companions in my life who have loved me, served me, and laid down their lives for me. May the love and friendship between David and Jonathan be a model for all healthy, faith-centered relationships in my life. Like Jonathan, permit me to cast my lot with you even when it may mean breaking with family and friends who do not understand your ways. Help me keep my focus on doing your will despite the cost and may my joy be reflective of my friendship and love of you, my God and my all. Amen.

QUOTE

"One of the most fun nights I've had was the retirement party of my college baseball coach, Frank Giannone. Coach retired 15 years after I finished school and after 30 plus years in the dugout.

The amount of alumni that came was staggering. Former players coming from all over the New York area, Florida, Arizona, Texas, California, all to celebrate the career of one man that meant so much to all of us. Spanning 30 years many of us didn't know players from before or after our time on the team, but it didn't matter. We were all LIU Blackbird baseball players. The stories flowed, many of them very similar about Coach. The same lines, the same jokes, the same drills. Friendships were forged, addresses and phone numbers were exchanged between people who had never met before that night because simply we were Blackbirds and that means that this guy must be a good guy. It's amazing to know that any of us can call another for help and can count on it coming. The power of a teammate."

—*Brad Keely*[7]

REFLECTION QUESTIONS

Who have been some of your faithful friends over the years? Do they share similar qualities and characteristics?

How does the knowledge that you have a trusted and loving friend help you through the ups and downs of life?

When have you made a stand for your faith or for a friend? Was it an easy or difficult experience?

Would you characterize your relationship with God as a friendship? What elements are similar or dissimilar?

LOVE CONNECTION

Reflect on some of the friendships that have sustained you in life and pray for those people and let them know you were thinking about them in a tangible way.

chapter eight

RUTH AND NAOMI
LOVE LIGHTS THE WAY

Sometimes when disaster strikes we don't think of what we should do but rather to whom we should turn for help. Our initial inclination may be to do nothing at all, to wallow in self-pity. We may get angry at God and demand answers about our misfortune. Thankfully, most of us have the blessing of people in our lives that will know what to do next, who will help get us back on our feet. These are the people we remember. While we may not recall the exact words they said, we remember their presence. The story of Ruth and Naomi is one such example of being there for another in their time of need. These two remarkable women will provide for each other out of friendship and love, all founded on their unyielding trust in God.

Early on in the book of Ruth we learn that Naomi is an Israelite who marries a Moabite man and goes to live in his homeland. They have two sons who marry Moabite women. Quite suddenly and without explanation, Naomi's husband and two sons die, leaving her alone with her two daughters-in-law, Ruth and Orpah. This was truly a bitter situation in a culture and age when most women relied on a father, husband, or son for material support.

These three women found themselves widowed with no children to support them.

There are few words more beautiful than these in the Hebrew Scriptures spoken from Ruth to Naomi:

> Do not press me to leave you
>> or to turn back from following you!
> Where you go, I will go;
>> Where you lodge, I will lodge;
> your people shall be my people,
>> and your God my God.
> Where you die, I will die—
>> there will I be buried.
> May the Lord do thus and so to me,
>> and more as well,
> if even death parts me from you! (Ruth 1:16–17)

In these short verses we get a glimpse into the depth of the ten-year relationship they shared. The loud weeping and sobbing as Naomi tried to bid Ruth and Orpah farewell speaks to the love these women must have shared throughout the years. How many meals had they prepared together? How many journeys through the intense heat of the desert did they endure? How many times did they talk and laugh as they made their way to the well? How many days did they spend practicing the rites of purification together?

Naomi is concerned for the younger women who found themselves without husbands and had no protection and no security for their future. Being older and wiser, she realizes what may lay ahead for her daughters-in-law, and she wants the best for each of them. No mention is made of her concern for her own welfare, no mention of her own plight. Her only concern is for these two women; this is a love that seeks the good of the other.

While they are still of childbearing age, Naomi calls for them to return to their own homeland to marry again. Naomi's blessing seeks the Lord's kindness upon them as she prays that he will grant them husbands so that they may find rest.

Affectionately she kisses each of them and the tears and sobbing commence. One can only imagine the questions that were running through their minds: What am I to do now? Where am I to go? God, where are you?

However, this is no ordinary, "goodbye and good luck" speech, for the Lord is involved. Naomi is faithful to the Lord! While it's reflected in her speech, "May the LORD deal kindly with you, as you have dealt with the dead and with me" (Ruth 1:8), it must have been evident in her everyday dealings as well. Naomi must have modeled in her own life, in her dealings with her family and with others that the Lord was in control. Her faithfulness to the God of Abraham, Isaac, and Jacob must have differentiated her from the others with whom these two Moabite women were used to dealing. Her faith in God was put into action through her love for Ruth and Orpah. What a wonderful mother-in-law indeed.

Ruth makes a decision that impacts her immediate future and will lead to the birth of King David and to Christ himself (Matthew 1:5 mentions Ruth in the genealogy of Jesus). She does not go back to her people and her ancestral god, but stays with Naomi who has the Lord as her God. There is a bond there that is greater than flesh, a bond of faith.

Ruth not only verbalizes her faith in saying, "your God my God," but it's apparent through her dwelling with Naomi, even in this time of bitterness, that her faith is a lived reality. Ruth's piety will be a sign for all peoples that God does indeed look at the heart. Ruth's outward action of devotion and her decision to follow Naomi will be rewarded.

It may seem reasonable and even advantageous to follow a person who has many possessions and riches, while quite another thing to abide with one stricken by misfortune. The latter seems to be the case with Naomi. She even pleads with her daughters-in-law to go their own way as she claims that, "...the hand of the Lord has turned against me" and "...the Almighty has dealt bitterly with me" (Ruth 1:13, 20). Yet it is clear that she sees the hand of the Lord at work in her life. It is by the hand of God that Naomi describes her misfortune which points to the fact that all things that befall us—good or bad—are permitted by God. Naomi will soon learn that while God is unpredictable, he is never unfaithful. The message sent in Proverbs rings true in Naomi's life, "Trust in the Lord with all your heart, and do not rely on your own insight. In all your ways acknowledge him, and he will make straight your paths" (Proverbs 3:5–6).

Naomi affectionately refers to Ruth as "my daughter." What comforting words these were to Ruth as she continued her journey of faith as a stranger in a strange land. After returning to her own village of Bethlehem, Naomi's concern turns to finding a suitable and pleasing home for her daughter-in-law, Ruth. Following Naomi's directions, we find Ruth gleaning—or gathering ears of grain together—in the field of Boaz, an upright and faithful man. Boaz recognizes Ruth's faithfulness to her mother-in-law, and recognizes her trust in God.

Boaz, a name that means "strength," is a kinsman of Naomi's family. He laid claim on her Ruth's late husband's estate by taking her his wife. Ruth bore him a son and the women of the town praised God in return, "Blessed be the Lord who has not left you this day without next-of-kin and may his name be renowned in Israel! He shall be to you a restorer of life and a nourisher of your old age; for your daughter-in-law who loves you, is more to you than seven sons..." (Ruth 4:14–15).

Ruth's love was offered freely, totally, and faithfully to Naomi and this love bore fruit for Ruth, Naomi, and the entire people of God. Ruth's son, Obed, became the father of Jesse, who was the father of David, the future king of Israel.

It may seem peculiar that this relatively short book about two women, one who was not even Jewish, was included in the Old Testament—the Hebrew Scriptures. This story of friendship, faithfulness, and love has at the heart dependence upon the Lord. Even when things seemed to be at their worst, God provided for these two women who cared deeply about one another. Through their friendship and faith God was made present.

God works through the unlikely hero, Ruth: a Moabite, a foreigner, a Gentile. He uses her as an example of faith and discipleship. God holds up Naomi as a woman of great faith, a woman of integrity, and a woman who loves the Lord. Their friendship and faith in God, and each other, continues to delight those who read their story. It challenges us to consider that God can work through others who may differ from us in many ways, to accomplish his will in our lives. It can test our view of friendship and remind us to be faithful to those we call friends in the good times, as well as the bad.

Just as he did through Ruth, can God be speaking to us through the faithfulness of another? Do we look for those who show the outward trappings of success, or do we look, like Ruth, at the heart and obedience of a person who has committed themselves to God? Even when disaster may strike, we must cling to our integrity in the way we handle distress, trusting that all things come from the Lord. As it was with these holy women, our faith may be challenged, but we should never allow it to be broken.

PRAYER

God of Abraham, Isaac, and Jacob, draw our hearts closer to you and to each other. Thank you for providing faithful friends who travel the journey of faith with me, often into the unknown. Open my eyes that I may see a glimpse of your love and faithfulness in my friends. I am grateful for your love on my journey, and while I may not know where I'm going, I know that you are with me each step of the way. Allow me to be an example to others so that I might lead them ever closer to you. Amen

QUOTE

"I met Caitlin when I was in 4th grade. She had just moved across the country from San Diego, California to a street only a few blocks away from mine in Edison, New Jersey. Caitlin is a year older than me but that never put a damper on things, we always had our ways around the age difference dilemma; sneaking to each other's side of the play ground, planning secret meetings in the bathroom, the quirks of little girls. This went on throughout our school careers, grade school, middle school, and high school. And before we knew it 2009 came around, Cate's last year of high school. Like most seniors, off she went to college. Only this time it wasn't in sneaking distance from each other, it was 3,000 miles away, back to sunny San Diego. In the beginning it was a strange feeling having the ability to talk to someone you care so much about and at the same time focus on the reality of the huge distance between you. It was as if someone was testing me, expecting me to not withstand the change. Once we were reunited I sat back and realized over these months I had learned a valuable lesson. There is nothing—no distance, no problem, no worry, no amount of money, which can break the bond and love of a true friendship."

—*Julia Scarola* (student, Coastal Carolina University)[8]

REFLECTION QUESTIONS

Have you ever encountered a desperate situation where you wondered, "What will I do next?" How did it feel at the time? Was there anyone who stepped up and offered help?

Have you ever met a person whom you believed was sent by God into your life? Was it a dramatic encounter or a subtle meeting?

Is there a person in your life that you would follow because of their faith in God? Do you think anyone would follow you because of your faith?

God's blessings often come in strange ways. Can you think of a situation where your own faithfulness or someone else's faithfulness to God or to you made all the difference?

LOVE CONNECTION

I will be faithful each day in my friendship with God. Where the Holy Spirit leads, I will follow.

chapter nine

TOBIAH AND SARAH
A MATCH MADE IN HEAVEN

God knows what he's doing. He may not always fill us in on the details, but God knows. We may intellectually consent to the idea that God first set things into motion and that ultimately there is a master plan to this life of ours. Often however, a little interior voice beckons us and whispers, "God has larger issues at hand than your happiness, let alone your love life!" Perhaps the years of waiting and hoping for the one to come along and sweep us off our feet frustrates us and we end up settling for less than what God had in store for us. The waiting can be the most difficult part.

The beautiful story of Tobiah and Sarah gives us an angel's-eye view of faithfulness and love from God's perspective. In fact, this story reveals that our love life and happiness are in fact very important to God because he ordains them. The book of Tobit reveals a God who loves us and who has a vision much larger than our own.

The book of Tobit begins with a pious Jew, Tobit, who is faithful to the covenant despite being exiled to the city of Nineveh after the fall of Samaria in 722 BC. He continues to follow the requirements of the Jewish law such as avoiding food sacrificed to idols, burying the dead, clothing the naked, and regularly giving alms to the poor. He does this while his own people disobey the Lord's commands. We learn that Tobit takes his faith in God so sincerely that he risks his very life in order to be faithful to the Lord. For him, faithfulness to the Torah is paramount. God honors Tobit's faithfulness by granting him the lofty position as purchasing agent under Shalmaneser, the ruler in Nineveh.

As Tobit continues to live his life of faith, he marries Anna, a woman of his own lineage, and they have a son named Tobiah. Tobit continues his works of charity during the Feast of Weeks, and for doing so, he is mocked by his own people. Tobit's faithfulness to God is highlighted again and again, even at personal loss and ridicule. How often do we equate personal wealth and success as a sign of God's blessing? On the contrary, for many of the biblical characters, suffering is the sign that they are doing God's will.

In a strange turn of events, Tobit goes outside to sleep near the wall of his courtyard and the "warm droppings" of some birds settled in his eyes resulting in total blindness. After four years of blindness, his prayer, recorded in chapter three of the book of Tobit, reveals his desire to die and to no longer hear the insults of others. He feels that he cannot endure the misery of life. This prayer provides a glimpse into the heart of Tobit and echoes in the depths of many people who have reached the end of their rope. They have been faithful. They have trusted God. Yet God seems to be so distant, absent. The waiting for an answer, a sign, or some indication that God is present is the hardest part and they begin to fall away from God. Thankfully, the book of Tobit faithfully records this prayer, perhaps to give us hope in the midst of our desperations, doubts, and struggles.

At that same time, a young woman named Sarah, prayed for death as well. Sarah, daughter of Raguel, had been married seven times, and on the evening of each honeymoon, an evil spirit named Asmodeus killed each and every husband. Can you imagine what husbands number three through seven were thinking when they married Sarah? In her anguish, Sarah considers hanging herself but decides against it because it will bring shame to her father. We are told that Sarah beautifully, "...pours out her prayer" before the Lord. Her inner torment and suffering find expression in prayer to God.

"At that very moment, the prayers of both of them were heard in the glorious presence of God" (Tobit 3:16). These magnificent words recorded in chapter three reveal that their prayers were indeed heard. When there was suffering, agony, or affliction Tobit and Sarah turned their eyes and hearts to God. God was well aware of their suffering and was about to answer their pleas in an extraordinary way. He sent the angel Raphael to heal them in their time of distress.

Tobit remembers a large amount of money he deposited in the town of Media with a man named Gabael. He sends his son Tobiah to the town after giving him strict instructions about giving alms and obeying the decrees of the Lord. The angel Raphael, disguised as a human named Azariah, becomes Tobiah's traveling companion. Anna is concerned that she will never see her son again for the road to Media is a dangerous one. In a tender moment Tobit says to her, "So, no such thought, do not worry about them, my love." These are comforting words of love from one who, while afflicted with blindness, can see the hand of God on the life of his son.

Making camp at nightfall near the banks of the Tigris River, Tobiah went down to the river to wash his feet when he was assailed by a large fish that bit down upon his foot. The angel told the boy to take hold of the fish and he hauled it ashore. Following the angel's instructions he cut out the gall, heart, and liver and kept them with him.

At this point you may be thinking, "What's going on here?" Fish liver, bird droppings, blindness, seven husbands killed on their wedding night, angels? This is in the Bible? Strange as it may seem, yes, it's in the Bible. While I concur that these things do sound strange, I wonder if some of the occurrences in our own lives aren't just as strange. I can think of accidents, funny incidents, confrontations, and just plain bizarre happenings in my own life that cause friends and strangers to shake their heads, smirk, and walk away mumbling, all the while being no less extraordinary than some of these incidents.

Tobiah hears reports that Sarah is his own kinswoman. She is described as, "sensible, courageous and very beautiful." News of the seven previous husbands dropping dead appears to have traveled around as one would most certainly expect. You can imagine the terror in any man who may have been interested in her. Common sense would dictate that marrying her would make them a statistic rather than a husband. The angel Raphael leads Tobiah to reason that Sarah would be an excellent wife for him considering she is from his lineage and that Tobiah's father desired that he should marry.

Despite Tobiah's objections, Raphael tells him to give no thought to the demon but rather to place the fish liver and fish heart on the embers of fire used for incense for it will ward off the evil spirit for, "...she was set apart for you before the world was made. You will save her and she will go with you" (Tobit 6:18). Raphael says, "Do not be afraid" and "do not worry." We then learn that Tobiah fell deeply in love with Sarah.

Sarah's father, Raguel, agrees to the marriage and has a wedding contract drawn up according to the decree of Moses. He then states that, "Your marriage to her has been decided in heaven." What joy these words must have brought to both Tobiah and Sarah. At last, their faith and trust in God was rewarded. Two hearts given to God are joined as one. As they entered the bridal chamber to join their bodies to what their voices had spoken, they begin to pray, "Blessed are you, O God..."

Raguel is a little less confident than one might expect, for he is digging a fresh grave for Tobiah. However, Tobiah is found to be asleep with his new bride and yes, he is breathing. Raguel too, opens his mouth in praise of God.

After a heartfelt farewell, the newlyweds return to Tobiah's home. Tobit and Anna welcome their son and accept Sarah with joy as their own daughter. At this juncture the angel Raphael reveals to them who he really is. Raphael says that it was he who, "...presented and read the record of your prayer before the glory of the Lord" (Tobit 12:11). Their response is quite natural; they fall down in fear. Raphael states quite humbly that he is not the one to receive any credit because it was the will of God, so he bids them to rise up and worship God. Tobit then composes a joyful song of praise, and the story closes with an exhortation to follow the commands of God.

The story of Tobiah and Sarah reveals that, while God's ways are not our ways and God's timing is not our timing, he does have a plan. He is intimately concerned about the details of our lives, and in particular, our love lives. Tobiah and Sarah both sought God's will first and foremost in their lives and God brought them together in a most magnificent way.

Whatever God does, he does beautifully and perfectly. God doesn't have another way of doing things. We, being made in God's image and likeness, have the same desire to express our love in a most perfect and beautiful way. While we may fall woefully short at times in expressing our love, it's still the mark for which we aim.

While Tobiah and Sarah are expecting to be married, they are focused on God. This clear observation is relevant for us today as we often seek our "beloved" apart from the will of God. As in this story, God can work with anything or anyone to bring about his will...even fish gall! Tobiah and Sarah allowed God to work in their lives, despite the complications that arose. In the end, these two were a match made in heaven.

PRAYER

Heavenly Father, increase our faith and confidence in your steadfast love for us. Assist us in entrusting ourselves into your eternal and good will, especially when we are at our darkest points. Saint Raphael, continue to assist single people in the discovery of their vocation, and if it is marriage, lead them to joyfully discover their spouse. Protect us from all harm and change our hearts so that we may joyfully accept that which is prepared for us in heaven. Saint Raphael, Tobias, and Sarah, pray for us. Amen

QUOTE

"If you follow the will of God, you know that in spite of all the terrible things that happen to you, you will never lose a final refuge. You know that the foundation of the world is love, so that even when no human being can or will help you, you may go on, trusting in the One who loves you."

—*Pope Benedict XVI*[9]

REFLECTION QUESTIONS

Can you think of any occurrences in your own life that are in fact stranger than fiction?

Tobit and Sarah found an expression for their agony in prayer. How has prayer helped you deal with suffering or confusion?

How have you or how can you include God in your love life?

Has anyone assisted you in life that may have been an angel in disguise?

LOVE CONNECTION
Be an angel to someone who is in search of their true love. Remind them not to worry, but to be faithful and to trust God in all things.

chapter ten

SONG OF SOLOMON
THE LOVER AND THE BELOVED

Let him kiss me with the kisses of his mouth!
For your love is better than wine,
   your anointing oils are fragrant,
your name is perfume poured out;
   therefore the maidens love you.
Draw me after you, let us make haste.
   The king has brought me into his chambers.
We will exult and rejoice in you;
   we will extol your love more than wine;
rightly do they love you. (Song of Solomon 1:2–4)

Yes, this is in the Bible!

It seems that these words would be more likely to appear in a steamy romance novel rather than in the inspired Word of God. Yet, they are the inspired Word of God! Their inclusion in the canon of the Old Testament was as controversial in the early church as it is now. The sexual, erotic nature of the lover and the beloved speaks to the power that sexuality stirs within us.

The Song of Solomon, or Song of Songs (literally meaning "the greatest song"), is a dialogue between two lovers extolling the beauty and nature of love in poetic form. The man is named "king" and "shepherd" while the woman is called "sister" and "bride." Their words give expression to their mutual desire for each other and the images are wrought throughout with sensual pleasure. The appeal to the senses abounds: touch, sound, sight, taste, and smell all come alive as the reader is intoxicated with perfumed oils, spices, fruits, flowers, trees, beds, and secret gardens.

Analogies and comparisons are used throughout the book to convey the depth and breadth of love's delights. "Your love is better than wine" (1:2,4, 4:10, 7:9), "fragrant perfumes" (1:3, 12; 3:6; 4:10), "the beloved's cheeks" (1:10; 5:13), "her eyes like doves" (1:15; 4:1), "her teeth like sheep" (4:2; 6:6), "the lover like a gazelle" (2:9, 17; 8:14), "the beloved's voice" (2:8,14, 8:13), "powerful Lebanon" (3:9; 4:8, 11, 15; 7:4) all evoke the senses and touch the heart.

Interestingly we find the woman speaking as freely and assertively as the man, a rarity in that time and culture. The woman is on equal footing with the man and on the lips of both can be found sensual praise and desire for the other. We are taken in by God's beautiful gift of eros—romantic and erotically stimulating love—and are drawn toward a deep union with the other person.

> I am a rose of Sharon,
>   a lily of the valleys.
> As a lily among brambles,
>   so is my love among maidens.
> As an apple tree among the trees of the wood,
>   so is my beloved among young men.
> With great delight I sat in his shadow,
>   and his fruit was sweet to my taste.
> He brought me to the banqueting house,
>   and his intention toward me was love.

Sustain me with raisins,
   refresh me with apples;
   for I am faint with love.
O that his left hand were under my head,
   and that his right hand embraced me!
I adjure you, O daughters of Jerusalem,
   by the gazelles or the wild does:
do not stir up or awaken love
   until it is ready!
The voice of my beloved!
   Look, he comes,
leaping upon the mountains,
   bounding over the hill. (Song of Solomon 2:1–8)

In the midst of the arousal there is a word of caution, "…not to stir up or awaken love until it is ready!" This phrase is repeated two other times throughout the poetic song. The physical union alone doesn't draw us as close as we desire. Eros, the sexual expression of love, in body alone can bring about selfishness, pain, and exploitation. The aftermath is far from what God desires for us to experience. Like with all gifts that God gives, when used separated from his will, the gift is stained by sin. The desire of these two lovers is more than just a sexual expression; it is a lifelong journey together in love.

Upon my bed at night
   I sought him whom my soul loves;
I sought him, but found him not;
   I called him, but he gave no answer.
"I will rise now and go about the city,
   in the streets and in the squares;
I will seek him whom my soul loves."
   I sought him, but found him not. (Song of Solomon 3:1–2)

The seeking, the longing, the laying awake thinking about the beloved through the night is beautifully articulated in these passages. The experience is common to everyone in the early stages of romantic love and attraction. The emptiness one feels when the other is not near, when physical intimacy cannot be expressed. The lover's voice is referred to four times and the allure of love that the voice stirs within is exhilarating.

> Set me as a seal upon your heart,
> > as a seal upon your arm;
> for love is strong as death,
> > passion fierce as the grave.
> Its flashes are flashes of fire,
> > a raging flame.
> Many waters cannot quench love,
> > neither can floods drown it.
> If one offered for love
> > all the wealth of one's house,
> > it would be utterly scorned. (Song of Solomon 8:6–7)

The power and unitive nature of love is exposed beautifully in the expression, "Set me as a seal on your heart." A seal was a distinctive form of identification that was worn around the neck with a cord. We read of Judah leaving his seal and cord with Tamar in Genesis 38:18 as a means of identification. To set one as a "seal upon your heart" is the outward expression for interior union with the other. Death was the greatest strength a person could know in the Old Testament; no one could escape its power for it pursued all people, from peasant to royalty. Love pursues the other with the ardor, fervor, and overwhelming strength in the same way that death pursues all. Love refuses to fail! Love reaches its zenith when it is described as "flashes of fire" and a "raging flame." No longer is it a self-seeking plummet into the temporal intoxication of pleasure, but rather, a desire to sacrificially abandon self for the good of the other.

We should not be surprised that such words filled with explosive sexual imagery appear in the Bible. The Word of God is, after all, a true love story. Our sexuality is a beautiful gift that God sanctified by offering his first command to Adam and Eve to, "be fruitful and multiply" (Genesis 1:28). What is surprising is that there is no mention of God, the Torah, prayer, covenant, sin, Moses, the prophets, or the temple in the entirety of the book of Song of Solomon. These terms appear regularly across other texts in the Old Testament. While the omission of these words is interesting, it does not imply that God is not in the mix. Saint John says in 1 John 4:7–8 to "…love one another, because love is from God; everyone who loves is born of God and knows God. Whoever does not love does not know God, for God is love." Perhaps the name of God is not mentioned in the passages because he is already there, deep within the encounter with love. The lovers are free and faithful, seeking and longing for each other. There is no fear, only desire for union, which is where we find God.

The Song of Solomon provides beautiful images that reveal, on a spiritual level, the love God has for us. These holy passages speak in experiences and languages to which we can relate. God uses the marriage theme in describing the love for his people all throughout the Bible (see Hosea 2:16–24, Jeremiah 2:2, Isaiah 54:4–8, and Isaiah 62:5). When describing divine love, words fall short. Thus, God directs us to images that help us to experience love on a level we can comprehend.

The two words that sum up this book for me are found on the lips of Jesus, as well as in any chapel of the Missionaries of Charity, founded by Mother Teresa: "I thirst." Mother Teresa revealed the depth of God's love for us by daily satiating this

Divine's thirst for souls with her charitable work. The Song of Solomon is a point of departure for reflection on our relationship with God who longs to take us into the desert and speak to our heart of his love.

PRAYER

Living God, Eternal and Faithful Love, pursue me all the days of my life. Draw me into your heart and in silence let me hear your voice calling me by name into the mystery of your love. Beloved Lord, help me not to fear in your presence for perfect love casts out all fear. Help me to love and receive love with total abandon. Satiate my thirst and let me find rest and peace. Then will my true self emerge and my joy radiate like the noonday sun. Amen.

QUOTE

"Love is our true destiny. We do not find the meaning of life by ourselves alone—we find it with another."

—*Thomas Merton*[10]

REFLECTION QUESTIONS

What strikes you first about the Song of Solomon? Are you surprised that such a romantic and erotic book is in the Bible?

Are you comfortable with the image of God as a pursuing lover? What other images of God speak to you ?

Who has loved you in ways that got your attention?

How is the development of a healthy sexuality affirmed in the Song of Solomon?

LOVE CONNECTION

See yourself as the apple of God's eye and ask God for the grace to experience in a tangible way his personal love for you.

LOVE

IN

THE

NEW

TESTAMENT

Volumes have been written about the word we translate as *love* in the pages of the New Testament. There are three main Greek translations for the word *love*: *agape, philia,* and *eros.* Pope Benedict XVI beautifully explores the depths and Christian understanding of these words in his encyclical letter *Deus Caritas Est*—a must-read for any serious Christian seeking to grasp the meaning of love—which is ultimately an encounter with a person: Jesus Christ.

The word *eros* most often refers to sexual love, a passionate longing for the other, and sexual attraction. *Eros* appears only twice in the Greek translation of the Old Testament and is not used in the New Testament at all. The writers of the New Testament most likely avoided using this word because of its association with cultic practices where temple prostitutes were engaged to manifest some sort of divine madness. *Eros* has been redeemed by Christianity, and when the body and soul are united, *eros* allows us to mirror the divine love God has for us.

Philia means friendship, or a bond that holds people together, and it is the only other word besides *agape* used in the New Testament for love. The word typifies the love that Jesus has for his disciples.

The writers of the New Testament choose the Greek word *agape*, to exemplify what was meant by Christian love. This is the prevailing word used for love in the New Testament. One observation that sometimes gets overlooked is that Jesus' primary language was not Greek, so he never used this word. However, the entire New Testament was written in Greek, so the authors used this word almost exclusively to convey Jesus' teaching on love. As Christianity moved westward from Palestine to Hellenized Asia Minor to Greece to Rome, the language moved as well, and so we come across the word *agape*.

Agape is less precise than *eros* or *philia*, and that may be the reason that the authors of the New Testament chose to use it. The word *agape*, and words derived from it, appear 341 times in the New Testament and can be found in every single New Testament book. So what then are we to make of this all-important word? Simply put, the essence of *agape* is sacrificial, other-centered, unconditional care for neighbor and enemy.

In the parable of the Good Samaritan, the Samaritan felt no physical attraction for the wounded man, no *eros*. He was not an acquaintance, family member, or friend with anything in common, no *philia*. What motivated the Samaritan to stop and get involved in the life of a man who was wounded, stripped, and left half-dead on the roadside? It was *agape*. The Samaritan saw a human being in crisis and preferred to do what was best for the victim at a great cost to himself. So the understanding of *agape* is not found in linguistic study of Greek, but rather in the pages of the Bible itself. As the parable of the Good Samarian makes clear, even when we don't find the word *love* in the story, love is right there staring us in the face.

While studying the Greek and Hebrew origins of words can be beneficial, we must realize that words have limitations. For the Christian, love is defined not so much by words but by the actions of Jesus who is the Word of God made flesh (John 1:14). One could say that love became flesh in the person of Jesus and dwelt among us. So love is a matter of the will involving both our head and our heart. We have the freedom to love or not to love. We can choose who we love, what we love, when we love, as well as how we love. For the Christian, we will be known as followers of Jesus not so much by the recitation of our creed but by the quality of our love. "I give you a new commandment, that you love one another. Just as I have loved you, you also should love one another. By this everyone will know that you are my disciples, if you have love for one another" (John 13:34–35).

Saint John tells us in his first letter that, "There is no fear in love, but perfect love casts out fear; for fear has to do with punishment, and whoever fears has not reached perfection in love. We love because he first loved us" (1 John 4:18–19). *Agape* ultimately has its origin in God, and those who experience this love in the person of Jesus Christ desire to share it with others.

chapter eleven

ZECHARIAH AND ELIZABETH
FAITHFUL LOVE, EXPECTANT FAITH

Zechariah and Elizabeth are introduced within the first few verses in the Gospel of Luke and they are the first married couple we encounter in Luke's Gospel. Zechariah was from the priestly division of Abijah, and Elizabeth was from the daughters of Aaron. Right off the bat we are informed that this couple has some pretty good lineage and family history. We also learn that, "Both of them were righteous before God, living blamelessly according to all the commandments and regulations of the Lord" (Luke 1:6). Not a bad reference for the résumé!

However, the next verse informs us that they were without children and Elizabeth was barren and advanced in years, which was a severe blow and humbling to any husband and wife who longed for children. In their culture, such a childless state could be viewed as a punishment by God and due reason for a divorce. However, Zechariah and Elizabeth began their journey together, believing in God's providential love and in the traditions of Israel, and they were going to finish their days united in marriage.

Elizabeth and Zechariah were righteous. They knew God. They were well trained and faithful to the covenant. They observed the commandments and they did so blamelessly. They prayed to God for a child, and their prayers were answered. We learn that, while Zechariah was officiating in the sanctuary of the Lord while burning the incense, their prayer had been heard by the Lord. Their prayer reveals that they yearned for a child of their own. The years of waiting and praying without a child did not deter them from their religious duties and they did not abandon the faith. They trusted in the Lord.

Because of their faithfulness we can assume that Elizabeth and Zechariah were familiar with salvation history; how God worked throughout history to reveal himself and redeem his people. I'm sure their thoughts turned to other barren women whom God made fruitful by gifting them with a child. I'm sure they also considered women like Sarah, Rebekah, Rachel, Samson's mother, and Hannah, the mother of the prophet Samuel, all whom played a vital role in the history of Israel by bearing sons. In times before the Ten Commandments some of these barren couples took matters into their own hands and turned to the cultural practice of taking another woman as a second wife to produce a male heir. In taking a second wife, these couples revealed a lack of trust in the power of God to bring about a child. Zechariah and Elizabeth, however, are faithful to each other and to God, even in challenging times when their hopes and desires are not immediately fulfilled. They relied upon prayer.

The Shema Yisrael, or Shema, is a beautiful Jewish prayer found in Deuteronomy 6:4 and is familiar to Jews and Christians alike; "Hear, O Israel: The LORD is our God, the LORD alone" Per God's commandment to his people, the prayer is offered by observant Jews twice a day; once upon rising in the morning and then again when retiring to bed in the evening. It is the first prayer a Jewish child is taught, and the last prayer offered by a faithful Jew before leaving this earth. The words of the Shema are contained in the mezuzah which is affixed to the doorpost of Jewish homes. This beautiful prayer which Jesus knew and prayed, (see Mark 12:28–34), was well known to Zechariah and Elizabeth. While the depth of meaning and application of this prayer is worthy of study, the first word of God's command is to "hear."

One of the challenges that confront people in all ages is this ability to hear—to really listen to one another and to God. Our technology-savvy world allows us the ability to e-mail, text, and instant message one another, but does real communication occur? Are we just spewing information with no true dialogue taking place? While God can certainly respond quicker than an instant message, we are often not interested in listening on his schedule. Many saints have written that silence is necessary in order to enter more deeply into the spiritual life. While this silence may at first seem like the absence of God, it takes us one step closer to understanding God's first language—silence. It is in silence that God is fully present.

God's four hundred-year silence is broken with a simple announcement to Zechariah and then to Mary. When the angel speaks to Zechariah his first words are, "Do not be afraid." While the presence of an angel—Gabriel no less—causes Zechariah to be struck with fear, the words, "Do not be afraid" are pretty straightforward and audible. The years of silence, the years waiting for an answer to their deep longing for a child, found reply from God to this faithful son and daughter of Israel.

After learning that his wife is with child Zechariah offers a song of praise, which is a walk through salvation history. He mentions the God of Israel, Abraham, David, the covenant, salvation, holiness, mercy, redemption, righteousness, forgiveness of sin, and the tender mercy of God. Zechariah knew the story, but it seems he did not expect that he and Elizabeth would play such a prominent role in the history of Israel. Their faithfulness to the covenant, to temple worship, and to each other reveals a life of sacrifice, service, and commitment, which is the essence of love.

The love between Zechariah and Elizabeth was a mature love that trusted in God's providence. Their eyes were opened to God who is unpredictable, but never unfaithful. Their eyes were opened to God doing something new in their lives, despite their advanced age. Their eyes were opened to see Gabriel, to see their son John, to see Mary, the Handmaid of the Lord, and to see Jesus, the promise and desire of all nations. Zechariah's mouth was opened that he may proclaim God's faithfulness and love.

PRAYER

Lord God, out of silence you spoke to Zechariah and announced good news. Grant us the grace to be faithful and obedient in the midst of the doubt, confusion, and uncertainty that life can bring. Let your presence be known to couples who have difficulty conceiving a child, and give all couples generous hearts, open to new life. Remind us not to be afraid of anything in this life for you are with us each step of the way. God of surprises, come quickly. Amen.

QUOTE

"Everything comes from love, all is ordained for the salvation of man; God does nothing without this goal in mind."

—*Saint Catherine of Siena*[11]

REFLECTION QUESTIONS

Zechariah experienced God in a place of worship. Have you ever experienced the presence of God in an exceptional way during worship? What was it about the experience that stands out?

In what ways are you faithful to God as a couple? Is it more difficult when life doesn't turn out like you planned or is it during those times that your faith unites you?

Are you comfortable with silence?

Are there any places where you can get away and enjoy silence? Have you encountered God in those places?

LOVE CONNECTION
Make it a daily priority to have time alone and in silence with God, not asking for anything, but just being present with him.

chapter twelve

MARY AND SAINT JOSEPH
SILENT WITNESSES TO LOVE

Very little is revealed about Joseph in the pages of the Gospels. While he is mentioned by name eighteen times, he is a man without words, but certainly not without witness. He stands as silent as the marble statues that depict his image. Most of his earthly life is shrouded in mystery. It's unknown how he died; nonetheless we do get a glimpse at how he lived, and in those few references we find a man who loved Mary and Jesus sacrificially.

When we come across Joseph in the Gospels of Saint Matthew and Saint Luke we find a man who loved God, loved his wife, and loved Jesus. His silence is not to be confused with indifference, for we observe his actions almost exclusively in the midst of crisis. His passionate, yet costly demonstration of protective love remains the model for all fathers and husbands down through the ages, and for ages to come. The marriage between Mary and Joseph gives us insight into both spousal and parental love.

When we first meet Mary in the Gospel of Matthew she is introduced in relation to Joseph, to whom she is betrothed. We learn that Joseph is a righteous man, honorable and in a right relationship with God. However, Joseph faces an immediate crisis when

Mary is found to be with child. Joseph had plans to divorce her quietly before the marriage so as not to expose Mary to the punishments of the law, but God had other plans. He spoke to Joseph in a dream and told him to stay with Mary, and Joseph was obedient to God's word. Joseph didn't break one of the most violated commands in Scripture: Do not be afraid! In strength and obedience to God he took Mary as his wife.

Libraries are filled with what has been written about Mary: virgin, wife, and mother. Mary, like all mothers, was there from the beginning. From the first movements of the child in her womb she desired to share her joy with Elizabeth and Zechariah, and praised God for her pregnancy, the fulfillment of God's Word and the hope of all mankind. Joseph was present too at those first kicks within her womb, and together this Holy Family modeled love through Mary's openness to life and through Joseph's obedience.

The next time we encounter Mary and Joseph, in Matthew's Gospel, they are faced with yet another crisis. Herod has plans to destroy the newborn king and so, "Joseph got up, took the child and his mother by night, and went to Egypt, and remained there until the death of Herod" (Matthew 2:14–15). Joseph is obedient and displays unconditional spousal love in caring for Mary and in protecting Jesus. He went at night, without a plan, without knowing the language, without his tools and, like most men, without directions! His love was evident in his actions and in each step of his journey toward Egypt, all for the sake of his family.

Joseph, ever obedient to the voice of God, returns from Egypt but decides to make their home in Nazareth. Herod's son Archelaus was ruling his father's territory and it would again put Jesus in danger. Joseph did whatever necessary in order to keep his wife and child safe.

We read in Luke's Gospel that Mary "…treasured these things in her heart." I'm sure that Saint Joseph was right up there at the top of her list. Here is man who is faithful and obedient to God. He remains steady in the face of a crisis, and he is faithful to his wife through it all. The descriptions and metaphors Jesus uses in his ministry based in and around the home are full of healthy domestic images, which must reflect the upbringing and love he experienced in his home in Nazareth.

We finally see Joseph with Mary in Jerusalem in the midst of yet another crisis; their child is lost. Together as one they seek Jesus and locate him in the temple. No words of anger escape the lips of Joseph, though Mary gives voice to their concern, "Child, why have you treated us like this? Look, your father and I have been searching for you in great anxiety" (Luke 2:48). In the midst of this crisis Mary and Joseph seek their child together and find him in a place of worship.

It's easy to picture Jesus sitting by Joseph's feet in the workshop, observing the love and care in which Joseph crafted his latest project. The chisel and hammer twisted and turned, fashioning the wood, resulting in a work that was both functional and artistic. Joseph's presence with his son must have impacted Jesus as any father influences his child. And what peace Mary must have felt, for what can be more assuring to a woman than a man who loves their child? I can imagine Joseph raising the hammer high and then bringing it down with a loud whack, and then another, and another. Then, turning to Jesus, he motions him over and with an outstretched arm says, "Now it's your turn, come, give it a try." As we reflect for a moment on the love and care that Jesus put into crafting his parables and his teaching, that were both functional and beautiful, we can see the image of God—his heavenly Father, and the reflection of Joseph—his earthly father.

A marriage brings with it the promise of fidelity, "for better or for worse, for richer or for poorer, in sickness and in health." Mary and Joseph's love stood the test of time and the trials of life.

Together they were united in trust in God's providence, united in the tender loving care of Jesus. Their spousal and parental love continues to be a model for believers, and challenges couples to be faithful to God and one another.

PRAYER

Saint Joseph and Mary, intercede on behalf of married couples and strengthen their faith and commitment to your Son, our Lord, Jesus. For through a solid faith in Christ and love grounded in the sacrament of matrimony, they can stand witness to the divine love that comes from God alone. May Saint Joseph's attentiveness to the Word of God strengthen and encourage men today to take a stand for marriage and family life, which is in crisis. We ask this in Jesus' name and under the protection of Mary, Mother of God, Mother of the church, and Mother of us all. Amen.

QUOTE

"Saint Joseph is a man of great spirit. He is great in faith, not because he speaks his own words, but above all because he listens to the words of the Living God. He listens in silence. And his heart ceaselessly perseveres in the readiness to accept the Truth contained in the word of the Living God."

—*Pope John Paul II*[12]

REFLECTION QUESTIONS

The Holy Family has been depicted in art thousands of times throughout the ages. Do you have any favorite images of Saint Joseph or of the Holy Family?

The idea of being a "holy" family seems out of reach for many and so they would never compare themselves to the Holy Family of Nazareth. What elements make up a healthy family and in what way is your family holy?

Who has been present to you in times of crisis? What difference did they make?

Mary and Saint Joseph offered their lives to God and to Jesus. How have those who serve God blessed you, and how has serving God been a blessing to you?

LOVE CONNECTION
Ask the Holy Spirit to make you more attentive to the mothers and fathers who stand together in times of crisis.

chapter thirteen

JESUS AND THE "SINFUL WOMAN"
A LOVE THAT POURS OUT ALL

The story of the sinful woman anointing Jesus' feet with her tears and perfume is one of the most beautiful love stories in the New Testament. Far exceeding the love stories found in cheap romance novels or made-for-TV specials, this love story is profound, costly, and continues to touch the heart and soul of all who hear it. Despite her silence, the woman, who is merely identified as the "sinful woman," displays a deep and abiding love for Jesus.

Jesus accepted the invitation of Simon, a Pharisee, to dine in his home. Hospitality is legendary in the Middle East and it was an honor to be able to host a party for Jesus, a young Galilean rabbi, who had a reputation as a great teacher and miracle-worker. It would be customary to offer a kiss of peace upon entry to the home (2 Samuel 15:5, 19:39; Matthew 26:49), a bowl of water to wash the dust off a guest's feet and, depending on the wealth of the host, scented olive oil to anoint the guest's hair (Psalm 23:5b, 45:7, 92:10, Amos 6:6). Customary as it was, it was not required of the host, but Jesus notes the absence of such rituals.

One of the keys to visualizing this story is understanding that Jesus "reclined" at table. The Greek word for recline is *anaklínome,* which means "to lie down." This typical Middle Eastern style of dining had the guests arranged around a triclinium, a three-sided table close to the floor, reclining on their left arm and supported by cushions, leaving their right hand free to feed themselves, their feet outstretched behind them.

It is into this house that a woman enters and makes straight for Jesus' outstretched feet. While she was not an invited guest, she enters. It was not uncommon for uninvited guests to enter into a house where they knew a scholar, a teacher of the law, was present, in order to listen to his teaching.

What happens next is extraordinary, for every head in the room would have turned and every jaw would have dropped in disbelief. The sinful woman makes her way toward Jesus' feet and weeping, she begins to bathe his feet with her tears. She then lets down her hair, which would have been covered, to wipe them. She then kisses Jesus' feet and proceeds to pour out ointment from an alabaster jar onto them. The woman's actions are one of the most lavish displays of public affection given to Jesus in his earthly ministry.

A woman's hair was, and still is, considered a "private part" in much of the Middle East, and is revealed only to her husband on their wedding night. In this remarkable encounter we see her letting down her hair to Jesus in public, an act of fidelity, affection, and commitment. She touches him tenderly and kisses his feet, another act of humility and affection. Finally, she anoints his feet with the ointment: lavish love poured out in the home.

It would not be a stretch to presume that this woman was a prostitute. Simon identifies her as a "sinful woman" and the clue as to her sin lies in the alabaster flask, for it was not uncommon for prostitutes to anoint their partners with ointment and costly perfume. It is understood that the woman had some amount of wealth and was likely successful at her former trade as the alabaster flask was an expensive import from Egypt.

What bothered Simon was not necessarily the touching of Jesus but rather who was touching him. Simon seems to define a prophet as someone who avoids sinners, while Jesus defines a prophet, through his actions, as someone who shows love to sinners and accepts their loving response.

Why the outpouring of love for this Galilean rabbi? Jesus provides the answer, "...I tell you, her sins, which were many, have been forgiven; hence she has shown great love" (Luke 7:47). Because she has received forgiveness of her sins, she demonstrates great love. This is a bold statement as to the divinity of Jesus because only God can forgive sin. Jesus accepts her outward display of love and praises her for it, another bold statement about Jesus' position. We are reminded of another nameless, silent woman, Peter's mother-in-law, who also served Jesus after receiving his touch of healing.

Jesus is not afraid to defend this sinful woman who wiped and kissed and anointed him repeatedly. Her reputation was not important to Jesus. He sees a woman who was broken, burdened by her sin, yet a woman created in the image of God, created to love and to be loved. Now that's social justice! Jesus is willing to take an unpopular stance and even challenges Simon in his own home shrewdly through a parable in order to defend her actions. He gave voice to the voiceless in language that stung Simon to the core. Her actions of honoring Jesus are in stark contrast to Simon's omissions.

The only acceptable response to love is love. This woman, now forgiven, whole, overflowing with the love of Jesus, poured out her former way of life at the feet of her Lord.

The story ends with Jesus acknowledging her faith and assuring her of his forgiveness while directing her to, "Go in peace." This peace is more than just an interior disposition of being free from anxiety and guilt, which undoubtedly flooded her whole being, but rather it conveys blessing and prosperity and wholeness from one Jew to another. Jesus restored her once again to the community, and welcomed her back into the friendship of God's chosen people.

PRAYER

Lord God, send your Holy Spirit in our hearts that we may have the wisdom to know what to pour out at your feet. Purify us from all that separates us from you so that we may reflect your image and likeness. Let us humbly approach you in the sacrament of reconciliation and let our reply be like this humble, unnamed woman who served and adored the very body of Christ. Through adoration and service to the poor may our response be as beautiful as hers. We pray this in Jesus' name. Amen.

QUOTE

"You know well enough that Our Lord does not look so much at the greatness of our actions, nor even at their difficulty, but at the love with which we do them."

—*Saint Thérèse of Lisieux*[13]

REFLECTION QUESTIONS

Have you ever been disrespected like Jesus was at the dinner party? How did it feel and how did you respond?

Jesus was not afraid to confront injustice in a way that was both effective and creative. Have you ever taken a stand in defense of a person or a cause? Did it cost you anything?

This woman poured out her former way of life at the feet of Jesus. Do you feel you can do this today? Besides the sacrament of reconciliation, are there any effective practices you employ to help "pour out" life's difficulties?

The forgiveness this woman experienced caused her to act. How can you translate your faith into daily action?

LOVE CONNECTION

Give the gift of yourself and time to Jesus and spend ten minutes a day with him in prayer.

chapter fourteen

SAINT PAUL AND BARNABAS
*STRENGTHENED AND
ENCOURAGED IN LOVE*

Some people are permanently linked to one another: Abbot and Costello, Lennon and McCartney, Lewis and Clark, and Simon and Garfunkel, just to name a few. It's difficult to think of one without the other. In the New Testament it would be difficult to find a closer pair than Barnabas and Paul; they were attached at the hip.

If you search for Barnabas in the Acts of the Apostles and the letters of Saint Paul you will find him referenced thirty-four times. Of those thirty-four mentions, twenty-nine appear in the Acts of the Apostles. When we first read of him we are told that his previous name was Joseph, but the apostles renamed him Barnabas, meaning "Son of Encouragement" (Acts 4:36). In Greek the name is *Paraklesis*, which can mean encouragement, exhortation, consolation or comfort. The function and character of a person who encourages should not be thought of any less than other roles in the community, for remember that the Holy Spirit is referred to as the *Parakletos*, Advocate and Comforter.

It is Barnabas who introduces Saul, whose name would later be changed to Paul, to the apostles after his experience with the Risen Jesus. Perhaps Barnabas recognized the genuineness of Paul's conversion and discerns that Paul too is called to be an apostle (Acts 9:26–27). We next find Barnabas going to Tarsus to seek out Paul and then he takes him to Antioch after hearing that the Gentiles are receiving the Holy Spirit (Acts 11:25–26). Barnabas knows of Paul's mission to the Gentiles and he knows Paul needs to be in Antioch to see what God is doing among the people. Barnabas is the early link between the Gentiles and Paul, and encourages Paul to be where God needs him.

The next twenty-five times we read about Barnabas in the Acts of the Apostles we see his name mentioned immediately before Paul thirteen times, and immediately after Paul twelve times. Barnabas and Paul, and Paul and Barnabas! Two peas in a pod! Remarkably, it is only the initial description of Barnabas in Acts 4:36 that we find him mentioned without reference to Paul.

The love and respect these men had for one another is obvious in the way they labored, preached, taught, and suffered together for the gospel. In conjugal love there is a union of bodies, in this *philia* love, there is a union of souls and purpose. In ministry they were equals, each sharing in the proclamation of the Good News. Luke sums up Barnabas' character by saying, "He was a good man, full of the Holy Spirit and of faith" (Acts 11:24). Luke then follows this endorsement with an important addendum: Wherever Barnabas went, "a great many people were added to the Lord."

What an impact Barnabas must have had in the early formation of Paul's theology and pastoral manner while Paul was in his company. He was not afraid to stand by him in times of turmoil. While the believers in Jerusalem were suspicious of him he extended his hand in kindness. No doubt Barnabas helped and encouraged Paul to become all that God had called him to be. Could Paul have reached his potential without a friend like Barnabas in his life? The power of the Holy Spirit was operative in Paul's life, just as it is in our own. Also powerful is the encouragement offered to us by others, for it is truly a gift that comes in the flesh from the Spirit. Saint Paul and Saint Peter saw encouragement as vital to those involved in living out the faith, as is evidenced in the following passages:

> I am sending him to you for this very purpose, to let you know how we are, and to encourage your hearts. (Ephesians 6:22)

> And we sent Timothy, our brother and coworker for God in proclaiming the gospel of Christ, to strengthen and encourage you for the sake of your faith.... (1 Thessalonians 3:2)

> Therefore encourage one another.... (1 Thessalonians 4:18)

> Proclaim the message; be persistent whether the time is favorable or unfavorable; convince, rebuke, and encourage, with the utmost patience in teaching. (2 Timothy 4:2)

> Through Silvanus, whom I consider a faithful brother, I have written this short letter to encourage you to testify that this is the true grace of God. Stand fast in it. (1 Peter 5:12)

The love between Barnabas and Paul did suffer a setback.

> After some days Paul said to Barnabas, "Come, let us return and visit the believers in every city where we proclaimed the word of the Lord and see how they are doing." Barnabas wanted to take with them John called Mark. But Paul decided not to take with them one who had deserted them in Pamphylia and had not accompanied them in the work. The disagreement became so sharp that they parted company; Barnabas took Mark with him and sailed away to Cyprus. (Acts 15:36–39)

The argument was not over an interpretation of what they believed about Jesus or their mission, but rather about John Mark, the cousin of Barnabas who had deserted them on a previous mission. Barnabas wanted to take him with them on their next journey. Barnabas was willing to give John Mark a second chance.

I'm drawn to the fact that Barnabas was willing to give John Mark a second chance. Perhaps the decision to part was best for John Mark, whom some scholars suggest is the author of the Gospel of Saint Mark. Years later, Paul finds the formerly useless Mark "useful," as revealed in the apostle's concluding epistle. "Get Mark and bring him with you, for he is useful in my ministering" (2 Timothy 4:11). And in Colossians 4:10, one observes that the once-rejected young worker was commended, and the Colossian saints were asked to be receptive to him. "Aristarchus my fellow prisoner greets you, as does Mark the cousin of Barnabas, concerning whom you have received instructions—if he comes to you, welcome him." So, while Barnabas and Paul were not always of one mind regarding John Mark, they were still of one purpose: spreading the gospel.

I'm glad that Luke, the author of the Acts of the Apostles, decided to include this somewhat embarrassing episode in the life of these two great missionaries. It reveals that we can have differences with those we love and confirms that real reconciliation can take place, which is a challenge for many today.

In the end Barnabas and Paul labored together and displayed a love based on encouragement and sacrifice. May we be encouraged by their love and friendship and recognize those who lead us closer to God through both word and action.

PRAYER

Jesus our Good Shepherd, help us to show love by encouraging one another. Send forth your Holy Spirit to encourage us in our life of faith when the road seems too difficult, or when we feel that we are traveling this road all alone. Lead us to friendships that encourage and build us up. When there is despair or depression, let the light of your love be my guide, for you will be ever at my side. In Jesus' name we pray. Amen.

QUOTE

"What does love look like? It has the hands to help others. It has the feet to hasten to the poor and needy. It has eyes to see misery and want. It has the ears to hear the sighs and sorrows of men. That is what love looks like."

—*Saint Augustine*[14]

REFLECTION QUESTIONS

Who is the most encouraging person you know?

Has there been anyone in your life who had the right words at the right time?

Have you ever "caught" a person doing the right thing and encouraged them? In what ways is it easier to criticize than to encourage?

How might rephrasing a critical remark make all the difference in how we interact with one another?

How can you be a "Barnabas" in your marriage, family, amongst friends, and in the workplace?

LOVE CONNECTION

Make an effort to encourage someone today. Allow yourself time to hear God's affirming word to you in the silence of your heart and through others.

chapter fifteen

PAUL, SILAS, AND LYDIA
LOVE TAKES A BEATING

Saint Paul was not a Lone Ranger in his ministry. He had many coworkers who labored with him in his missionary journeys. Some of these Christians who assisted Paul, and a few who even opened their homes to him, were men and women whose names are recorded in the pages of Scripture: Timothy, Titus, Epaphroditus, Euodia, Syntyche, Clement, Philemon, Apphia, Archippus, Phoebe, Prisca and Aquila, Epaphras, Mark, Aristarchus, Demas, Luke, Sosthenes, and Apollos, to name and honor just a few.

Silas is one such disciple of Jesus who is a coworker with Saint Paul. Silas, or Silvanus as he is also called, is mentioned fourteen times in the New Testament. Silas was sent with Saint Paul and Barnabas to Antioch to communicate the decisions of the Council of Jerusalem to the Gentile community in Syria. When Paul and Barnabas argued over John Mark, Silas was chosen by Paul to accompany him on his second missionary journey to Syria, Cilicia, and Macedonia. Silas was with Paul at Philippi and was involved with Paul when a riot broke out in Thessalonica, which drove the two from the city to Beroea. Paul left Silas there but rejoined him at Corinth. Silas is mentioned with Timothy by Paul and helped him preach at Corinth. Silas is also mentioned as the man through whom Peter communicated, and is considered by some scholars to be the author of that epistle. Catholic tradition says he was the first bishop of Corinth and that he died in Macedonia.

It is these two men, Paul and Silas, who take a beating for the sake of love. It is recorded in the Acts of the Apostles that,

> On the sabbath day we went outside the gate by the river, where we supposed there was a place of prayer; and we sat down and spoke to the women who had gathered there. A certain woman named Lydia, a worshipper of God, was listening to us; she was from the city of Thyatira and a dealer in purple cloth. The Lord opened her heart to listen eagerly to what was said by Paul. When she and her household were baptized, she urged us, say-ing, "If you have judged me to be faithful to the Lord, come and stay at my home." And she prevailed upon us. (Acts 16:13–15)

Lydia is considered the first European convert to Christianity. We read that she is a worshiper of God and is open to hearing what Paul has to say about Jesus. She believes and was baptized along with her husband, and she begins to serve them and bids them to stay at her house.

While in the city, Paul heads toward the place of prayer and is confronted by a "slave-girl" who has the "spirit of divination." This ability to tell fortunes brought a great deal of money to her owners. She would follow Paul and the disciples and would, "...cry out, 'These men are slaves of the Most High God, who proclaim to you a way of salvation. She kept doing this for many days. But Paul, very much annoyed, turned and said to the spirit, 'I order you in the name of Jesus Christ to come out of her.' And it came out that very hour" (Acts 16:17–18).

We might assume that this would be the end of the account, but the story takes a turn because her owners have now lost a valu-able source of income.

But when her owners saw that their hope of making money was gone, they seized Paul and Silas and dragged them into the marketplace before the authorities. When they had brought them before the magistrates, they said, "These men are disturbing our city; they are Jews and are advocating customs that are not lawful for us as Romans to adopt or observe." The crowd joined in attacking them, and the magistrates had them stripped of their clothing and ordered them to be beaten with rods. After they had given them a severe flogging, they threw them into prison and ordered the jailer to keep them securely. Following these instructions, he put them in the innermost cell and fastened their feet in the stocks. (Acts 16:19–24)

It's difficult to imagine the humiliation and physical beating that Paul and Silas went through. Stripped, beaten, flogged, and chained like beasts—welcome to missionary life with Saint Paul!

I find it amazing that that Paul and Silas kept quiet about one very important thing, namely, that they were Roman citizens. You see, they did not have to take that beating that day. All they had to do was open their mouths and say, "Hold it right there! You cannot beat us or treat us this way until we have had a trial, for we are Roman citizens." If they said this, the beating would have stopped instantly and it would have scared the soldiers half to death.

Why didn't they open their mouths at this injustice? Why didn't they claim their rights as Roman citizens? Why did they suffer this humiliation? They did it because of love!

An earthquake rocks the prison while Paul and Silas are praying in the middle of the night and the magistrates decide to let them go early next morning.

But Paul replied, "They have beaten us in public, uncondemned, men who are Roman citizens, and have thrown us into prison;

and now are they going to discharge us in secret? Certainly not! Let them come and take us out themselves." The police reported these words to the magistrates, and they were afraid when they heard that they were Roman citizens; so they came and apologized to them. And they took them out and asked them to leave the city. After leaving the prison they went to Lydia's home; and when they had seen and encouraged the brothers and sisters there, they departed. (Acts 16:37–40)

Before departing the city and leaving the prison they went to Lydia's home because it appears that Paul and Silas wanted to send a message to the police and magistrates of that town. They could have very easily made a case against those who imprisoned them, but instead they took their beating and upon their release the magistrates and police accompany Paul and Silas to Lydia's home.

What is the message being sent by Paul and Silas? Why didn't they just get out of there as quickly as possible? They are implicitly communicating that Lydia and her household were their friends. If they heard of anything happening to them or their new Christian community, their memory of how the town beat and imprisoned Roman citizens may return—therefore, hands off!

Paul and Silas heroically defend these new believers and take a beating that they did not deserve. They gave their very bodies over to be beaten in order to protect Lydia and her household. They took the unjust punishment honorably, just as their Lord had done.

Real love demonstrates the willingness to suffer, even in the midst of injustice. I wonder how Lydia and her household responded to the protective love that was shown to them by Paul and Silas. Did Lydia think, "Wow, who are these men who took a beating and suffered humiliation for us and for our benefit and safety?" I wonder what the soldiers thought of this little Christian community that loved one another so much that they were willing to take a beating. No doubt the preaching of these early disciples had a great impact on many. But it was their actions, as expressed through self-sacrifice and suffering, that revealed the depth of their love, their *agape*, much like their Master.

PRAYER

Lord Jesus, what Paul and Silas demonstrated by their sacrificial love they learned from you who took away our sins through your unjust and humbling death on the cross. Allow us to stand against injustice, but give us your heart and mind so that we may suffer with dignity and honor. Paul and Silas, pray for us and be our guide in our missionary efforts to share Christ's love with others, especially with those at home, with our loved ones, and with those who suffer injustice. We ask this through Christ our Lord. Amen.

QUOTE

"Charity is our great virtue because it is the great virtue of Jesus ...The love of God means the love of our neighbor. There is no better evidence, no truer proof of a great love of God, than a great love of our neighbor. Love of our neighbor is proven in patience and in trial, in the corporal and spiritual works of mercy. A treatment of our neighbor that is inconsiderate, harsh, un-brotherly or un-sisterly is un-Christlike, and argues a great want of the love of God."

—Father Thomas A. Judge[15]

REFLECTION QUESTIONS

Who has been a faithful friend to you over the years? Has that friendship ever been tested by trial or crisis?

Injustice often stays in our memory for a long time. Has there been a time when you were treated unfairly? How does your reaction compare with that of Silas and Paul?

Lydia must have been shocked by the costly demonstration of love undertaken for her and the church in her home. Has there been a time when someone shocked you with unexpected love?

Saint Paul's life was filled with beatings and suffering. How does your faith give you the strength to get through life's sufferings?

LOVE CONNECTION

Take time to thank Jesus for his costly love for you and seek out opportunities to reach out to others with the same costly love.

chapter sixteen

PAUL, ONESIMUS, AND PHILEMON
LOVE UNCHAINED

In the ancient world people could become slaves for a number of reasons. Through birth, children born to slaves were considered slaves. Prisoners of war could be sold as slaves, while others even sold themselves into slavery to pay off debts. Slavery was not uncommon in New Testament times. Jesus himself mentions the practice of a master selling his servant, his servant's wife, children, and property in the parable of the unforgiving servant. Saint Paul uses the image of slavery in his writing eighteen times, and refers to himself as a slave of Christ Jesus numerous times (Romans 1:1, Galatians 1:10, Philemon 1:1, Titus 1:1). Saint Paul taught that the Christian slave is the Lord's, and strongly proclaimed the spiritual equality of slave and free person. "For whoever was called in the Lord as a slave is a freed person belonging to the Lord, just as whoever was free when called is a slave of Christ. You were bought with a price; do not become slaves of human masters. In whatever condition you were called, brothers and sisters, there remain with God" (1 Corinthians 7:22–24).

However, the reality of being a slave is different from using slavery as an analogy. It is this reality that challenges a man named

Philemon, a follower of Jesus. Philemon is the owner of a man named Onesimus, whose name means "beneficial" and "useful." Will love have the final say in how Philemon treats his slave?

One of the ironies of this short letter by Saint Paul is that he himself is imprisoned at the time he writes his impassioned plea for the freedom of his "child in faith," Onesimus. Philemon was a slave owner who also hosted the Eucharistic celebration in his home, the common practice in the early years of Christianity. Philemon most likely heard Saint Paul's preaching and became a Christian. Saint Paul mentions in this letter that, "I have indeed received much joy and encouragement from your love, because the hearts of the saints have been refreshed through you, my brother" (Philemon 1:7). It is evidenced by this letter that Philemon was a dear and intimate friend to Saint Paul.

There are two schools of interpretation regarding the relationship of Onesimus, Philemon, and Saint Paul. The first suggests that Onesimus is a runaway slave who had taken something from his master, Philemon, only to later meet Saint Paul in prison and become a Christian. Paul then sends Onesimus back to his master pleading for Philemon to show mercy and leniency in his punishment of the slave. The second interpretation sees Onesimus as a slave sent by Philemon to help care for Paul in prison. Through contact with Saint Paul Onesimus converts to Christianity and yearns to stay with the saint and join him in his missionary activities. Accordingly, Saint Paul lovingly requests Philemon to do him this great favor and free Onesimus, who has now become a brother in Christ to Philemon, and a child in faith to Saint Paul.

Saint Paul had written persuasively on many occasions to the Christian communities that he founded. Of all his writings, his letter to the Galatians, perhaps, was his most forceful plea. Here, however, he uses the art of fatherly persuasion to gracefully ask Philemon to receive Onesimus as Saint Paul himself does, as a Christian brother and not as a slave.

> For this reason, though I am bold enough in Christ to command you to do your duty, yet I would rather appeal to you on the basis of love—and I, Paul, do this as an old man, and now also as a prisoner of Christ Jesus. I am appealing to you for my child, Onesimus, whose father I have become during my imprisonment. Formerly he was useless to you, but now he is indeed useful both to you and to me. I am sending him, that is, my own heart, back to you. (Philemon 1:8–12)

Saint Paul's appeal is on the basis of *agape*, the love that claims no rights for itself but rather seeks what is beneficial towards the other. Saint Paul first refers to Onesimus as, "my child" and doesn't refer to him a slave until verse sixteen of this twenty-five-verse letter. Philemon would have had to go against the norms of the culture to grant Saint Paul's request, yet Saint Paul assures him that Onesimus would now be useful to him as well.

While we don't know the outcome of Saint Paul's request, we do know the love that transformed Saul into Saint Paul was the same love that transformed Philemon into a beloved brother who refreshed the hearts of the believers. In the end of Saint Paul's letter to the Colossians we hear once more of Onesimus, "I have sent him [Tychicus] to you for this very purpose, so that you may know how we are and that he may encourage your hearts; he is coming with Onesimus, the faithful and beloved brother, who is one of you. They will tell you about everything here" (Colossians 4:8–9).

We can suppose that in addition to Tychicus and Onesimus telling the Colossians about the situation with Saint Paul, they also spoke of Philemon's love in treating Onesimus as a brother in the Lord. Now useful to one another, they both continued to spread the gospel of God's love.

PRAYER

Blessed be your Holy Name, Jesus, Lord and God, you humbled yourself and took the form of a slave in order to set us free. Thank you for the freedoms we have and help us to stand against all who would enslave others through human trafficking and unjust government systems. Help us to free those who are enslaved by sin, fear, and ignorance with our proclamation of the good news through word and deed. Direct our steps through prayer. May we never lose sight of the dignity of every human being and may we always be useful and beneficial in your service. We ask this in Jesus' name. Amen.

QUOTE

"The Church teaches us that mercy belongs to God. Let us implore him to bestow on us the spirit of mercy and compassion, so that we are filled with it and may never lose it. Only consider how much we ourselves are in need of mercy."

—*Saint Vincent de Paul*[16]

REFLECTION QUESTIONS

What are the first words that come to your mind when you hear the word "slavery?" Why does Saint Paul refer to himself as a slave? What are some similarities between slavery and being a disciple of Jesus?

Saint Paul saw that Onesimus was indeed "useful." Are there people in your life that make you wonder about their usefulness? How does our faith challenge the belief that some people are useless?

What gifts do you bring to your marriage, family, and parish community?

LOVE CONNECTION

Through the eyes of faith I will view all people as beneficial and created in the image and likeness of God.

chapter seventeen

JESUS, LAZARUS, MARY, AND MARTHA
A LOVE STRONGER THAN DEATH

It's not easy to mention the story of Lazarus without quickly jumping to the end where Jesus raises Lazarus from the dead. But before the movers pushed away the stone and before we hear Jesus calling Lazarus out of the tomb from death to life, from darkness into the light, we get a glimpse into this loving relationship that Jesus cultivated with Mary, Martha, and Lazarus. The death of Lazarus will call forth and reveal the depth of love that Jesus, Mary, Martha, and Lazarus shared.

> So the sisters sent a message to Jesus, "Lord, he whom you love is ill." But when Jesus heard it, he said, "This illness does not lead to death; rather it is for God's glory, so that the Son of God may be glorified through it." Accordingly, though Jesus loved Martha and her sister and Lazarus, after having heard that Lazarus was ill, he stayed two days longer in the place where he was. (John 11:3–6)

This news of a death of a loved one is not foreign to us. It is part of life, and as much as we may hate to hear the news, we can't escape it. Jesus was not the first or last person to weep over the death of a friend. It is an experience to which most of us can relate. It matters not the circumstances surrounding the death of the loved one for the sense of loss, pain, and confusion can affect us deeply. Even when death may seem to be a blessing, the days and months that follow are often filled with weeping and mourning.

When Jesus receives the news about the death of his friend Lazarus, he responds to his disciples with words of faith and confidence in God's providence. However, when he faces the sorrow of Lazarus' two sisters he breaks down and weeps with them. So evident is Jesus' sorrow that the crowd reacts, "See how he loved him" (John 11:36).

What a beautiful scene; Jesus, Mary, and Martha together with the crowd weeping in each other's arms at the loss of a friend, a loved one. Leaning on each other and being present during a time of sadness and loss is often enough. The agony of separation that death brings in this life was experienced by Jesus who wept unashamedly with his friends. His knowledge that Lazarus would be raised from the dead in no way meant that Jesus was indifferent to human emotion. Our faith in God shouldn't prevent us from weeping at the losses and hardships we experience in life, for that's what God intended. Why else would we have tear ducts?

We read that Jesus delayed in his coming when he had heard that Lazarus was ill; "...he stayed two days longer in the place where he was" (John 11:6). Why did Jesus delay and allow his friend to die? Why did Jesus allow Lazarus' sisters to go through the agony of seeing their brother pass away when we are told that he did love him? Where is the love in the delay?

This is the point where faith enters in. Faith that Jesus knows what he's doing, even when the situation is dire. Mary and Martha both echo these sentiments and say, "Lord, if you had been here, my brother would not have died" (John 11:32).

However that is not where Martha's response ends, for her friendship with Jesus is not based on receiving blessings nor is her faith just an intellectual ascent to belief in God. She states beautifully and powerfully in her own voice that

> "...Lazarus will rise again in the resurrection on the last day."
> Jesus said to her, "I am the resurrection and the life. Those who
> believe in me, even though they die, will live, and everyone who
> lives and believes in me will never die. Do you believe this?" She
> said to him, "Yes, Lord, I believe that you are the Messiah, the
> Son of God, the one coming into the world." (John 11:24–27)

Martha's faith is in the person of Jesus. Her whole being testifies to this belief and in the way she addresses Jesus as "Lord," "Messiah," and "Son of God." Mary, too, recognizes Jesus is in control both by her words in addressing Jesus as "Lord" and by the fact that she knelt at his feet, a sign of worship and submissiveness to his will.

True friendship does not run or waver at the first problem that arises. Friendship and love are able to ask the hard questions without fear. We come to know our true friends specifically during the times of trial and hardship. The Proverbs remind us that "A friend loves at all times, and kinsfolk are born to share adversity" (Proverbs 17:17). The friendship and love of Mary and Martha did not wane even when Jesus delayed his arrival during the illness of their brother. And because of their faithfulness, these two women were present for one of the most memorable and remarkable miracles in the Gospels: Jesus raised Lazarus from the dead.

What were Lazarus' first words? What did Martha and Mary and Jesus say to him after the burial bands were unwrapped? Who did Lazarus embrace first? What was the reaction of those stone movers? How did Lazarus now approach life? Wouldn't you love to have been there? I can only imagine that no matter the words, the tears again flowed and the friends embraced.

Lazarus would die again an earthly death, but we know that love never ends. So too, our earthly existence is in fact, in faith, not our final destination for we are bound for glory, for eternal life! The love and friendship that we experience in this life with Jesus will continue for all eternity. While we struggle with friendships and what is required of friendship, it is all a preview for the ultimate friendship and love with Jesus in heaven where death does not have the last word and there will be no more sorrow or tears.

PRAYER

Heavenly Father, the fear of death grips of us all in one way or another. Remind us that those who die in faith are promised eternal life. When the death of family or friend touches us let us recall your words, "Do not be afraid," and help us remain faithful. Let our tears flow freely and may they be an outward sign of longing to be reunited in heaven. At times when we feel that you are absent from our suffering and pain and are delaying in your aid, help us see that nothing comes to us except through your hands and that love does have the final word. Amen.

QUOTE

"Recently my wife of fifteen years died of a sudden heart attack leaving me with four children, three girls ages 12, 11 and 6 and a boy age 10. This was a dramatic, life-changing event, but as I reflect on the story of Lazarus I am comforted. Like Jesus and Lazarus, my wife Kathy was my best friend. While we were opposites in many regards we both shared a strong faith in God.

When Jesus learned of Lazarus' death he knew he was dead and I can say that I knew that Kathy was going to die as well; my background in human anatomy and physiology led me to that conclusion while she lay in a coma. While the rest of my family and friends were praying for her recovery, I was seeking the Lord's strength to help me cope with the future. My main concern was and is raising our children.

I ask myself, why did Jesus wait for two days to return to Judea? Was it because he needed time to grieve alone or did he have prior commitments? As for me, I needed time alone. When the extended family came to the hospital to visit, I left to find a quiet space outside the hospital and found a cold park bench. During this time I grieved and more importantly I sought God's support and strength and focused on praying for my kids.

A year has since passed since Kathy's death and unlike Lazarus's rising from the dead; I am left with only fond memories of my friendship and love of Kathy and the hope of being reunited with her in Heaven. I stay strong while moving forward, raising and loving my children as we pick up the pieces of our life and place them oh so carefully together. We have become very close and do not take life or each other for granted. We live each day focusing on what God has given and not taken away. For this, our faith in our Lord Jesus Christ has become stronger."

—*John Gresco*[17]

REFLECTION QUESTIONS

What drives you to pray more earnestly: good news or bad?

Can you recall an event that caused you to question God's timing?

Suffering and death are very often the reason why people abandon their belief in God. Has your faith strengthened you in times of trial?

People of faith do question God's timing; yet still move forward in faith. What type of prayer helps keep you moving forward in your faith life?

LOVE CONNECTION

Allow yourself sufficient time to grieve life's losses. In faith and compassion, reach out to those who have suffered a loss, no matter how great or small.

chapter eighteen

PRISCILLA AND AQUILA
A COUPLE FOR CHRIST

There are approximately one hundred and fifty married men and women who are proclaimed saints or blesseds in the Catholic church. Some of these notable saints who were married include Peter, Thomas Moore, Elizabeth Ann Seton, Rita, and Juan Diego. Yet, there are few, if any, married couples that achieved sainthood as a pair. (It should be noted that every Christian is a saint according to the testimony of sacred Scripture; Acts 9:32; Romans 15:25; 31; Ephesians 1:1; Colossians 1:2; Jude 1:3, to name a few.) Yet, the distinction remains between calling ourselves saints and recognizing those who have lived a heroic life of faith and even martyrdom.

Aquila and Priscilla (also known as Prisca), are the first couple of the early church. While we are familiar with individual men and women who made an impact for Christ in the early Christian community, Priscilla and Aquila did so as a married couple. They loved each other and Christ, and they opened their home, hearts, and marriage to him. Their openness to the spirit of God, their mutual loyalty, their focus on the mission, their willingness to risk their necks, their teaching, and their hospitality are more than admirable. According to tradition they were both martyred on their return to Rome, most likely around the same time as Saint Paul.

Aquila and Priscilla were Jews who were forced to leave Rome when the Emperor Claudius forbade the Jews to live there, circa AD 49. They made their way to the city of Corinth and set up shop, for they were tentmakers by trade. It was while they were in Corinth that they met Saint Paul, who was also a tentmaker. There is no mention of their conversion by the preaching of Saint Paul so it is reasonable to suppose that they were already Christians, for there had been Christian communities in Rome from the earliest times.

Priscilla and Aquila then accompanied Saint Paul on his missionary journeys. They are both mentioned in greetings to the Christian community, "The churches of Asia send greetings. Aquila and Prisca, together with the church in their house, greet you warmly in the Lord" (1 Corinthians 16:19). They are also greeted by Saint Paul by way of letter in Romans 16:3, "Greet Prisca and Aquila, who work with me in Christ Jesus" and in 2 Timothy 4:19, "Greet Prisca and Aquila, and the household of Onesiphorus."

One of the beautiful aspects of their love for one another was that they were united in mission. Upon hearing the eloquent preaching of a man named Apollos in a synagogue in Ephesus, they learned that he only knew of the baptism of John (Acts 18:24–28). Priscilla and Aquila privately reached out to him and explained the way of God more accurately. One can imagine the excitement that this couple had in being privileged enough to call over this articulate and persuasive preacher to teach him more correctly. This meant that this formidable couple had the respect of the Christian community that allowed them to use their charism of teaching to instruct and guide. What a beautiful experience it must have been for Aquila and Priscilla to share the authentic teaching about Jesus with others as a couple.

In Saint Paul's letter to the Romans, he is writing to recommend a woman named Phoebe to the church in Rome (Romans 16:1–2). He then goes on to mention twenty-six people by name who he would like to send greetings. Who is first on his list? Prisca and Aquila. What does he say about them? "Greet Prisca and Aquila, my fellow workers in Christ Jesus, who risked their necks for my life, to whom not only I give thanks but all the churches of the Gentiles" (Romans 16:3–4). What a beautiful testimony to the love that Paul, Priscilla, and Aquila shared among themselves as they are united in the Lord and in the mission to spread the good news! There are many who may share in our ministries but few who are willing to risk their necks for us as Prisca and Aquila were for Saint Paul. The phrase, "risked their necks" is still used today in a figurative sense, but when Saint Paul was writing these words they had a very literal meaning. Death for the sake of the gospel was real possibility in those times. Great sacrifice, great love!

"The churches of Asia send greetings. Aquila and Prisca, together with the church in their house, greet you warmly in the Lord" (1 Corinthians 16:19). What a wonderful image of the church meeting in a home and celebrating the Eucharist, sharing their faith, Scripture, songs of praise, and a meal together. The hospitality, the warmth, and the intimacy in which to share faith and share life was initiated and brought about by this couple who opened up their home and their hearts to others.

What a beautiful example for lay couples today who have an opportunity to share their charism through their marriages. A married couple provides a witness to the church and to the world by expressing their faith and unity through a shared ministry. How often is the faith experience for a husband and a wife so different that a joint ministry is never a possibility? Perhaps husband

and wife are separated by distance and occupation, never having an opportunity to share in ministry together. Yet, Aquila and Priscilla shared their ministry together. With a union of spirit and vocation this holy couple encouraged the faithful!

Today's couples for Christ come together and serve in the parish community in a number of educational and service ministries, often opening up their homes to share the faith. No doubt that couples who share a ministry and belief in Christ can share with each other on a deeper, spiritual level.

PRAYER

God the Father, Son, and Holy Spirit, Bless those couples who have opened their hearts and homes to you. Bless married couples who are united in their mission to raise their children in the faith and who serve together in the church. May we be remembered for our love of Christ and our willingness to step out in faith and risk our necks for following your will. Priscilla and Aquila, pray for us. Amen.

QUOTE

"My wife and I work together—in preparing for a week and its details or in charting a course for several months. We've figured out after over a decade of marriage that we're better together. I think that we've also learned to not only accept one another's foibles but highlight our strengths. My wife, Cary, is an amazing starter while I tend to be a good finisher—it's taken us a while to learn this but we make it happen through our common faith in Christ and the details of daily life."

—*Mike Saint Pierre*[18]

REFLECTION QUESTIONS

Can you think of any married couples that have inspired your life as a Christian?

Why do you think the church has so few canonized married couples? What qualities should the church be looking for in married saints?

It's not the mind-set of most Catholic couples to think about having a ministry or mission together. What ministries could you embrace as a couple to better live out your vocation and baptismal commitment?

How can you encourage younger family members or couples preparing for marriage to have this ministry mind-set?

LOVE CONNECTION

I will pray with my spouse that God may lead us to a ministry that we can share together.

chapter nineteen

MARY MAGDALENE, PETER, AND JOHN
FINDING A WAY BACK INTO LOVE

The saying goes that a crisis doesn't build character, but rather reveals it. The same can be said of friendship. While the church has persevered through trials and scandals through the centuries, no such trial is equal to the one experienced by those first disciples: the Crucifixion and death of Jesus. Following the Crucifixion we read of three disciples arriving at the tomb early Sunday morning. These friends were looking for Jesus.

The reaction of these three disciples and friends of Jesus reflects many similar reactions to Jesus still prevalent today. The first one on the scene early Easter morning is Mary of Magdala. Mary showed up at the tomb looking for Jesus. After seeing that his body was not there, Mary runs to tell Simon Peter—the leader of the apostles—the news about the missing body of Jesus. Peter, too, sets out for the tomb—the same Peter who, not seventy-two hours earlier, had denied he knew Christ.

Finally, Mary of Magdala also tells the "beloved disciple" the news of the missing body of Jesus; he outruns Peter and arrives first at the tomb. This beloved disciple, who reclined with Jesus a few days before and who was present with the Mother of Jesus when the soldiers nailed her son to the cross, now finds himself at the entrance of the tomb. He waits for Peter to arrive and then follows Peter into the tomb.

While Mary Magdalene, Peter, and the beloved disciple all showed up at the tomb, the reaction of each of these three friends who loved Jesus is different and worth examining more closely, for it is love that brought them to the tomb.

Mary went seeking the dead body of Jesus and wondered where he was after seeing the stone rolled away. She says, "They have taken my Lord and I don't know where they laid him." Mary's words were grounded in the reality of the missing body of Jesus. Some friendships with Jesus ask the identical question, "Jesus, where are you?" We come seeking Jesus and are left wondering where he is. Mary came seeking and found Jesus, or more correctly, the Risen Lord found her.

Mary's love for Jesus is often romanticized in popular novels, movies, and in made-for-TV miniseries. The main motivation for this romantic conspiracy is based in financial interest rather than historical reality. For the love that Jesus had for Mary of Magdala, and the love she responded with, was not the sexual lust that bombards us from all directions in today's society. The love Mary responds to is a deep, unselfish love that the world tries so desperately to imitate. The worldly concept of cheap love and instant gratification is always found wanting, therefore it can never satiate our deepest desires. The love between Jesus and all disciples is a love best experienced, and not bogged down with words. It is a love initiated by God himself through the Son and Holy Spirit who calls each of us by name.

One might ask as Mary did: "Where is the body of Christ today?" There are a few ways of answering that question. First and foremost, the body of Jesus is found in every tabernacle, on every altar, in every Catholic church in the world. The Body of

Christ is found in the Eucharist. One can explain transubstantiation which occurs and we can read John chapter six and reflect on Jesus' very words, "My body is real flesh," but I've found it best not to explain but rather to experience him there in adoration and in reception of Holy Communion.

Second, the body of Christ is found in the poor and abandoned, in the marginalized and forgotten. Mother Teresa reminds us in a most beautiful way that he is present in the distressing disguise of the poorest of the poor.

The body of Christ is also found in the community of believers. Saul of Tarsus heard the words from Jesus on his way to Damascus, "Saul, Saul, why are you persecuting me?" Saul was persecuting the church, the body of Christ, which Jesus so intimately identifies with. In both of these examples we can find Christ today if we seek him as Mary did.

Peter seeks Jesus as well, yet he remains silent at the tomb. The missing body of Jesus is cause for reflection and speculation about what has taken place since his death. In encountering Peter throughout the Scriptures, rarely is he at a loss for words. Does he speak the wrong words? Yes. Are some words spoken at the wrong time? Yes. In this instance however, we find Peter at a loss for words. Peter's silence at the empty tomb points to the contemplative dimension of the believer that the Resurrection demands. Like the Eucharist, it's one thing to simply accept by faith the Resurrection and quite another to allow the power of the Resurrection to permeate our lives and transform it. Peter was transformed and strengthened by it.

I often wonder what went through the mind of Peter during this time. After all, he must have been racked with guilt knowing that he denied Christ three times. Jesus even predicted his denial and looked at him the moment the cock crowed. I wonder if the prediction of Jesus concerning the denial caused Peter to reflect on another prediction Jesus made: that he would be handed over, suffer, be crucified, and be raised on the third day. If the denial prediction of Jesus came true could not the Resurrection prediction be true as well?

Peter's friendship with Jesus does not end at the cross, but begins anew in the breaking of the bread. This was a friendship that would lead Peter himself to a cross in Rome some thirty or so years later. Peter was given something after the Resurrection that gave him the wisdom to make better choices and to guide the early church in its mission to spread the good news. He was given the Holy Spirit. This is the same Spirit that God offers us and desires to pour into us. It is the gift of himself. What better gift can a friend give than the gift of self? This Holy Spirit brings forth the gifts and fruits of the Spirit, which enable us to respond to God's love and to follow him wherever he may lead.

The beloved disciple entered the tomb, saw, and believed. Belief! What a wonderful response to a friend and to God. What was it that enabled John to see and believe? It was undoubtedly the love that Jesus had for him. This love gives the beloved disciple an insight that Peter did not have, for it enabled him to come to faith immediately when he entered and saw the empty tomb and the burial clothes laying aside. When a person is loved by another, they are able to see things in the other that no one else can see. The impact of seeing the empty tomb and believing the Resurrection extended into the rest of this disciple's life. He was never the same. He must have radiated the presence of God the same way Moses did when he came down from the mountain after encountering God face-to-face.

Maybe we can change places with these three friends of Jesus at the tomb early on that first day of the week after the Crucifixion. Maybe like Mary, we wonder, "Jesus, where are you?" Perhaps we're like Peter, quietly reflecting or speculating about what he heard and now saw and what this will mean for his life and future. I hope we can change places with the beloved disciple who saw and believed. If you are like me, maybe you're a combination of these three friends depending on your frame of mind and the situation at hand. I would love to boast that I am exactly like the beloved disciple, but I am, as so many of us, a work in progress.

Like the friends of Jesus who gathered around the tomb in search of the Savior, we can be assured that our seeking will not be in vain! Our friendship with Jesus will never be outdone by his generosity.

PRAYER

Risen Lord, we long to encounter you at every moment of our lives. Increase our faith and give us the eyes to see you in every person we encounter, especially in the poor and marginalized. Let us hear you speak our name in the quiet of our hearts. Give us the grace to recognize you so that we may see and believe more firmly. In all of our friendships draw us ever more closely to you so that we may experience the fullness of life that your death and Resurrection has won for all. Amen.

QUOTE

"My confidence is placed in God who does not need our help for accomplishing his designs. Our single endeavor should be to give ourselves to the work and to be faithful to him, and not to spoil his work by our shortcomings."

—*Saint Isaac Jogues, s.j.*[19]

REFLECTION QUESTIONS

Would it be correct to say that you found Jesus or that he found you? Why?

Which of the three disciples in this chapter best resembles you? What qualities do they have to which you can relate?

Where have you found Christ? Where has that revelation directed you?

What would you have said if Jesus turned to you and said your name as he did to Mary?

What impact do you think Peter's silence and contemplation had on his future role as leader of the church?

LOVE CONNECTION

Make a conscious effort to seek the face of Christ in others and ask the Holy Spirit to reveal the mission to which he has called you.

chapter twenty

JESUS AND PETER
CALLED AND COMMISSIONED

One interesting note about many Gospel characters is that they're known only by their ailment or sin. A few examples include the sinful woman in Luke 7, or the paralytic of Mark 2, or the man with the withered hand, Luke 6:6–11. The decision not to reveal their names perhaps saved them from embarrassment, but it also allowed the Gospel writer to focus on the actions of Jesus. Yet, there's something in me that would like to know more information and get a better picture of these nameless individuals.

Peter is one very important figure in whom we are allowed to see the good, the bad, and the ugly. Peter, always named first in any list of the apostles, was one of the first called by Christ on the shore of the Sea of Galilee. He was one of the first four apostles called and present at the Transfiguration of Jesus. He witnessed firsthand the healing of Jairus's daughter, the loaves and fish, and most, if not all, of the miracles of Jesus. Peter heard Jesus deliver his parables, was proclaimed "Rock" by his Lord, was rebuked by Jesus, and even walked on water for a little while…and then sank. What a wonderful and full life that we get to see of this man in the pages of the Gospels.

All four canonical Gospels recount Peter's presence at the Last Supper and his ensuing denial of his knowledge of Jesus. After the third time Peter denied Christ, the cock crowed and Peter went off and "wept bitterly" (Matthew 26:75). How devastating that must have been for Peter. He had responded boldly to the question put forth by Jesus: "Who do you say that I am?" by affirming, "You are the Messiah, the Son of the living God" (Matthew 16:15–16). Peter now finds himself alienated from Jesus through his threefold denial.

How would you feel if you were Jesus? He had taught Peter for three years and poured himself into Peter in every way a teacher can. What was Peter's response? Denial. Peter denies that he even knows Jesus. What options did Peter have after his shameful decision? Would he follow the route of Judas who turned on himself and committed suicide after his act of betrayal?

Thanks be to God we have the rest of the story recorded in the Gospel of Saint John 21:15–19:

> When they had finished breakfast, Jesus said to Simon Peter, "Simon son of John, do you love me more than these?" He said to him, "Yes, Lord; you know that I love you." Jesus said to him, "Feed my lambs." A second time he said to him, "Simon son of John, do you love me?" He said to him, "Yes, Lord; you know that I love you." Jesus said to him, "Tend my sheep." He said to him the third time, "Simon son of John, do you love me?" Peter felt hurt because he said to him the third time, "Do you love me?" And he said to him, "Lord, you know everything; you know that I love you." Jesus said to him, "Feed my sheep. Very truly, I tell you, when you were younger, you used to fasten your own belt and to go wherever you wished. But when you grow old, you will stretch out your hands, and someone else will fasten a belt around you and take you where you do not wish to go." (He said this to indicate the kind of death

by which he would glorify God.) After this he said to him,
"Follow me."

I don't believe it was Jesus who needed to hear the words, "Yes,
Lord; you know that I love you" but rather he knew Peter needed
to say them. Jesus gave him an opportunity to affirm his love and
then gave Peter authority of supreme shepherd over the whole
flock and never mentioned Peter's denial. How's that for love?

What a choice for the leader of the church: a man who knew
failure and had been given another chance. What a stark contrast
to our political system where any failure seems to automatically
discount a person from achieving a position of importance. Jesus
knew Peter had failed, but he knew that it was only a setback. He
didn't dismiss those who failed, nor does he do so today.

When reading the two letters we have in the New Testament
named for Saint Peter, we gain insight into the heart and mind of
a man who was head of the church and was called to give his very
life for Christ. The love and forgiveness freely given and received
between Jesus and Peter goes to the very heart of what the
Christian faith is all about.

Jesus' last recorded words to Peter are simple and profound:
"Follow me." These words are spoken to a man who knew his
own weaknesses and faults and who also knew Jesus would never
abandon him, despite his failings. They are also spoken to you and
me. May we follow Jesus' way of love and enter into the heart of
the Holy Trinity.

PRAYER

Lord Jesus, Chief Shepherd, you reign in heaven with all power
and glory. Your mercy allows us to have a second chance and to
begin anew at each misstep of our lives as we struggle to follow
your way of love. Holy Spirit, come! Enliven our spirituality and
may our love for you and for our neighbor be known to all

nations. Oh Comforter and Spirit of Truth, strengthen us in our faith that we may not stumble in your way of love. Allow us to imitate you in making all things new. May you, Jesus, reign on earth and in our hearts with mercy and love. We ask this through Christ the Good Shepherd and under the protection of Mary. Amen.

QUOTE

"Sometimes, in moments of self pity, we think of ourselves as complete losers. But that can't be true! Remember, even a stopped clock is right twice a day. In other words, no matter how bad things stand, we always have something to offer. But the question is this: The gifts you have, why were they given to you? The New Testament cries out on every page: The gifts you have are for the support and enhancement of the people around you. This is the way one must translate that concise and beautiful saying of Jesus: 'Love one another.'"

—Monsignor James Turro[20]

REFLECTION QUESTIONS

How do you react when a celebrity or public figure does something criminal or just plain embarrassing? Is there a sense of pleasure when they mess up?

We have all made bad decisions at one time or another. How would you feel if it were written about or publicized for all to see?

Peter didn't take Judas' route of self-destruction after his failure. What is your initial reaction to setbacks? Are you readily accepting of forgiveness or does it take you a while to move forward?

Have you ever considered giving another person the opportunity to say what needs to be said? If so, how did they react?

How do you make time to hear Jesus' words of forgiveness and affirmation in your life so that you can follow him?

LOVE CONNECTION

Tell Jesus of your love for him and ask the Holy Spirit to make your mission clear as you follow him in the providence of your daily life.

chapter twenty-one

FINAL THOUGHTS

As I write these final thoughts from my dining room table I can see my wife hovering over our newborn daughter, Abigail, with my six-year-old, Sophia, patting the baby's tummy while our two-and-a-half-year-old, Cataleen, stands behind them holding a burp cloth. It's wonderful to see the loving response a newborn can draw out of our family and especially our young children. The home, of course, is where it all begins for the home is the great school of love. While we are by no means a perfect family, we do believe that when love, as expressed through kind words and actions such as sacrifice, service, and selflessness is present in the home, then we will recognize it elsewhere.

In reflecting on these love stories in the Bible we can think about people we have loved and who have shown love to us. Love is, after all, what Jesus commands and for good reason. We need love. We need to give it generously and receive it humbly from the hands of God.

May God lead us to a deep, profound, and personal understanding of his love for us and may we, through the help of the Holy Spirit, abide in that love which brings peace.

notes

1. Pope Benedict XVI, Angelus, Solemnity of the Most Holy Trinity, Sunday, May 22, 2005. Available at www.vatican.va.
2. Saint Thomas Aquinas, available at www.brainyquote.com.
3. Pope John Paul II, quoted in *Pope John Paul II: A Collection of Newspaper Front Pages Selected by The Poynter Institute* (Kansas City: Andrews McMeel, 2005), p. 51.
4. Pope Benedict XVI, *God Is Love: Deus Caritas Est* (Washington, D.C.: USCCB, 2006), p.16.
5. Elizabeth Tartaglia, postulant, Sisters of Christian Charity. Quoted with permission of the author.
6. Amber Dolle, quoted with permission of the author.
7. Brad Keely, pitcher, LIU-Brooklyn Blackbirds Baseball '89–'92. Quoted with permission of the author.
8. Julia Scarola, quoted with permission of the author.
9. Pope Benedict XVI, *Jesus of Nazareth* (New York: Doubleday, 2007), p. 38.
10. Thomas Merton, quoted at www.no-nukes.org.
11. Saint Catherine of Siena, quoted at www.catholicculture.org.
12. Pope John Paul II, quoted at www.catholicnewsagency.com.
13. Saint Therese of Lisieux, quoted at www.ncregister.com.
14. Saint Augustine, quoted at www.catholic.org.
15. Father Thomas A. Judge, "Meditations" (self-published), p. 199.
16. Saint Vincent de Paul, quoted at www.chonline.org.
17. John Gresco, father and anatomy and physiology teacher. Quoted with permission of the author.

18. Mike Saint Pierre, husband, father, and president of Morris Catholic High School. Quoted with permission of the author.
19. Saint Isaac Jogues, S.J., quoted at www.americancatholic.org.
20. Monsignor James Turro, quoted in James Turro, *Conversion: Reflection on Life and Faith* (Allen, Tex.: Tabor, 1983).

ABOUT THE AUTHOR

ALLAN F. WRIGHT is a husband, father, teacher, and academic dean of evangelization for the diocese of Paterson, N.J. His previous book, *Jesus in the House: Gospel Reflections on Christ's Presence in the Home,* earned a first-place Catholic book award in the family life category from the Catholic Press Association of the United States and Canada. He lives in New Jersey, with his wife, Desiree, and three daughters. www.allanwright.org.